MW01166697

Men
are
Scum,
Women
are
Stupid

Men Are Scum, Women Are Stupid
Copyright © 2008 by Jared Kempton
Published by Partigen Publishing, LLC

For further information, please contact:
www.jaredkempton.com

Book design by:
Arbor Books
19 Spear Rd. Suite 301
Ramsey, NJ 07446
www.arborbooks.net

Printed in the United States of America

Men Are Scum, Women Are Stupid
Jared Kempton

1. Title 2. Author 3. Relationships

Library of Congress Control Number: 2008929108

ISBN-10: 0-9818031-0-5
ISBN-13: 978-0-9818031-0-4

Jared Kempton

Partigen Publishing, LLC

Table of Contents

I want to dedicate this book to the wonderful women that have touched my life—particularly my wife, my mother, my sisters, and each of my grandmothers.

Also, thank you Noel for instigating this book. I hope it's what you were looking for.

Finally, a special thanks to all of my friends, family, and students who encouraged me and believed in me. It's because of you that this book reached completion.

About the Illustrators

Brandie Dziegiel

Brandie has loved art since she was young, and took every opportunity to study and try different forms of art all the way through secondary school. Brandie joined the Coast Guard after graduating from high school, but plans to continue studying art while serving and protecting her country. She hopes to be a professional illustrator and art teacher when she graduates from university.

Rob Ewing

When not working on illustrations or his own art, Rob works as an assistant activities coordinator at a nursing home in New Mexico. He uses his talents to brighten the atmosphere there with his artwork, as well as singing and playing the guitar. Rob studied art at the University of New Mexico.

Introduction

Do Dogs Feel Used?

As humans, I'm sure that we would like to think that we are more intelligent than dogs, but when it comes to love and relationships, I have my doubts. Think about it. When dogs reach a certain age, they become obsessed with a desire to mate. For the males, this means that they will mate with any female (or any object, for that matter) that will stop long enough to let them. On the females' part, some are picky and some are not. Whatever the case, the male gets his pleasure and splits, and the female is left alone to give birth and raise the puppies.

The process is very similar for humans. When we reach a certain age, new and exciting hormones kick in, causing us to think about the opposite sex in a way we never have before. For girls, this means a desire for companionship and mutual caring. For guys, this means a desire for sex. Like their canine counterparts, pubescent males have one basic objective on their minds: sexual

gratification. The only difference between guys and dogs, really, is that guys prefer their partners less hairy. The result is that guys and girls get together, guys get what they want, and the girls are left alone.

While such a system may work out great for dogs, it doesn't tend to go so smoothly for humans. While humans and dogs may be biologically similar, emotionally we are not. Female dogs are fine with never building emotional bonds with sexual partners, and they rarely stay up at night crying because "he never called back." The human mind and heart is not wired that way. For most of us, our greatest joys come from caring relationships with other people. Likewise, our greatest sorrows come from feeling used or abandoned. The result is that, unlike dogs, we *do* feel hurt when we are betrayed by those whom we thought we could trust.

The greatest mystery is this: after all of these years of evolution where we have progressed far ahead of the animal kingdom in almost every aspect of development, why do we still behave like dumb animals when it comes to sex and relationships? I believe that half of the problem lies with men. They, however, have no reason to change the animalistic sexual behavior of the human race, because it works out really well for them: all pleasure and no responsibility. I'm also going to go out on a limb and guess that the other half of the problem lies with women, which is who this book is for.

So if you're the type of girl who likes the excitement of every stray that crosses your path, close this book, find one on preventing STD's, and keep dating dogs. But if you are a woman who is tired of being treated like a dog, I believe this book can help.

Chapter One

Men are Scum

Men are scum. This may seem like a gross generalization, but in general, men are gross. Despite all the romantic notions that men or women may have about how men really are, the fact remains that nature has pretty much made them all one way: Hormone crazed animals bent on blessing as much of the planet as possible with their genetic code. Like any other male animal on this planet, the foremost thought on the untrained human male's mind is sex.

Some may argue that this is not true of all men. Sometimes men are more concerned with food and/or sports. On occasion this is true, but for all practical purposes, men are mainly concerned with sex.

This is not to say that all adult males are walking around only thinking about sex. I estimate that only 98.7% of adult males walk around in a hormone induced zombie trance of lust. For every thousand men, 13 of

them are rationally thinking gentlemen. We will get to those thirteen later. For now, let's examine the other 987 men.

It probably seems impossible to you that such a high percentage of the men are Jerks. You probably think that you have just been unlucky and found the few that looked nice but were actually Jerks. However, luck (or the lack thereof) had nothing to do with this. Mathematically speaking, the odds are truly against you. The problem is that it doesn't seem that way. This is because men, like all other predators in nature, are masters of camouflage.

We live in a society that has certain rules and codes of conduct. For men to be successful, they have to learn to live, at least to a certain extent, within these rules. This is part of the taming of the natural man. Men learn not to burp in public, not to pick their nose, not to hit when they get mad, to take showers when they stink, to brush their teeth, not to mix lights and darks in the wash, etc. They also learn that they can't have their way with women anytime they want. There are rules to interacting with the opposite sex, and to be successful, you have to know and manipulate those rules. For instance, men learn that women enjoy flowers and compliments, so they shower them with flowers and compliments. This is not because they think flowers are nice, or because they are generous with praise, it is because they have learned that this is how they can get what they want: sex.

This makes dating very difficult for women. They are looking for men with certain qualities—kind, considerate, good with children, faithful, hard working, stable, polite, courteous, patient, smart, etc. Men know this. So they act like they have all of those qualities. They will continue to act like they have those qualities until they feel that their prey is sufficiently hooked. It's a lot like fishing. Girls, like fish, won't just swallow anything floating in the water. They are looking for something specific—in this case, a worm. So the fisherman disguises his hook to look

like a worm. He lets the fish come in close and inspect. He waits patiently until the fish decides to go for it. And then, once the fish (or girl) makes the commitment, that's when it (or she) gets the Jerk. The hook is embedded, and , they proceed to get played by the fisherman. In dating terms, as soon as the woman has committed herself sufficiently to the relationship, she will get the Jerk instead of the gentleman she thought she had. Just in case you aren't caught up on guy lingo, "sufficiently committed" means "willing to have sex." This is all they want out of the relationship. And just like a fisherman who doesn't need the fish, as soon as they catch one and play it in, they will throw it back in the water for another fisherman, and proceed to try and catch yet another.

Not surprisingly, like fisherman, men tend to compare their 'trophy catches.' They brag and exaggerate and challenge each other to see who can net the most and the best fish. This is the nature of men. This is difficult to believe for most women, for two reasons. One, women aren't that way in general. Two, women rarely see men in their natural habitat behaving like the animals they are. For men, the above scenario is completely plausible, because they know it is true. They know that is how they are, and they have seen all of the other men acting the same way.

Let me share two examples from my observations of men when they are uninhibited by social mores. First, I played football in High School. The school I attended was in a very religious town of 1,800 people. Almost everyone went to the same church, and everyone knew each other. The young men of this community knew that they were always under the watchful eye of one adult or another. Also, most of them were fairly active in the local church group. These were fine young men—the type that any mother would approve of her daughter dating. In public they would not swear, they would help old women with their packages, and they would open the door for any woman.

However, in the football locker room there were no adults and no girls watching them. They were in the company of their pals, and shared a special camaraderie with each other. In the locker room, the conversations always turned dirty. These weren't bad guys. In fact, most of them intended on treating women right and even waiting until they were married to have sex, but in that environment they would stop holding back, and all they would talk about was sex. For those who didn't venture to that extreme, there was still the discussion of kissing, and how they felt cheated if they took a girl to dinner and didn't get a kiss. If they had dated a girl for a couple weeks, and she wouldn't make out with them, they were upset. In fact, it was made completely clear that the thing they really wanted was physical gratification—not the friendship or long-term relationship. They thought of girls in a purely physical manner. Of all the people in that locker room, there were only a couple of young men who didn't stoop to that level of thought and behavior. Again, I want to point out that this was among guys that were generally trying to be good.

My second observation is from the 75-man open barracks that I lived in while in the Army. I would never repeat the discussions that went on there, but I will say this: most of the conversations were about women, and all of those conversations were about some form of sexual activity. Some of these guys were (seemingly) perfect gentlemen outside the barracks. I remember one in particular who looked like he had a great relationship with his girlfriend. One night, someone told him his girlfriend was hot, and made some sort of sexual remark about her. He wasn't offended. Rather, he bragged about some of their intimate moments. Then he complained about how jealous she was whenever he talked to other girls. He felt she should be more trusting since they had been dating for over a year. Five minutes later he was discussing another girl he had slept with earlier that week. I was the only one in the room that found this disturbing.

I know that I have painted a dark picture of men, but you must believe me. I am a man. I know what I'm talking about, and I don't think that I can make this point clear enough: Men are scum. They are Jerks. All they want is sex. Women are objects to them—objects to be used for personal satisfaction, and casually discarded when something more enticing comes along.

Except for the 13 that I mentioned earlier. These thirteen men are what I will call 'Nice Guys'. Let me define a 'Nice Guy': A Nice Guy is a man who has the self-discipline to think of things besides sex. He cares about people. He is the guy that only wants one true love, and when he finds her, he will be faithful. He wouldn't ever use a girl. He might not be perfect, but he would never intentionally hurt a woman. He is the one who respects a woman for who she is, not for what she can give him. Nice Guys are not abusive—physically or emotionally. Nice Guys do nice things because they are nice, not because they want something in return. Nice Guys want companionship, a long-term relationship, someone that they can love for the rest of their lives. Nice Guys have spent their lives disciplining their minds so that they have control over their hormones. Though they were born with the same desires and motivations of other men, they have learned to control them in order to pursue those goals that they consider more worthy and pure.

This is a pretty strict definition, hence the fact that it excludes 987 out of 1,000 men. For a woman searching for that 'one in a million perfect guy' (or 13 in a thousand, as the case may be) this creates a two-fold challenge. One, how does she defend herself from all of the Jerks? Two, how does she find a genuinely nice guy if he is so rare? Hopefully in the chapters that follow, I will be able to answer those questions.

Chapter Two

Women are Stupid

Let me begin by clarifying the title of this chapter. This is a book about dating, so when I say women are stupid, I am building that stereotype within the context of dating. Women can be brilliant engineers, lawyers, or doctors, but when it comes to dating and men, they are very slow learners.

I can't blame women for their initial miscalculations and poor decisions in dating men. I blame the romance novel industry, fairy tales, Hollywood, and nature. All of these things seem to contribute to women having the following false notions:

1. Love conquers all. All you need is love. Love is all that matters. There is a dozen ways of phrasing this, but no matter how you phrase it, it is still wrong.

2. Some men are Jerks, but behind each Jerk is a long line of Knights in Shining Armor just waiting to rescue a damsel in distress.

3. Even the depraved, carnal man will change if he falls in love with the right girl.

4. In return for men giving women chocolate, flowers, compliments, dinner, etc., women should give men sex.

Every good book needs a conspiracy theory, so here is mine. Who wrote the fairy tales? Men. Who owns most of the publishing companies? Men. Hollywood producers and directors are primarily what gender? Men.

There is an unspoken agreement among men to never tell women what's going on. I could digress into a long discussion about the feminist movement and who it really benefits, but then I wouldn't have any material for a sequel, so I'll just say this: Men are controlling women's perceptions of what love and romance should be like. Men have a great gig going, and there is an alliance among them to not mess it up. Any dissenters (like me) are social outcasts, and therefore not popular enough for girls to listen to. Besides, who believes the occasional naysayer when men are so obviously gentlemanly and dreamy in the movies?

That is why I don't blame women for their first mistakes with men. In this Man's World, they stand little chance. What I do blame women for is making the same mistakes over and over and over and over and over again. Not only will one woman repeatedly make the same mistake, but it seems that she does little to pass any lessons learned onto the next generation, because women have been making the same mistakes for quite a while now. All of the evidence is in front of them that men are scum. In fact, they frequently lament that fact to each other and to men. But they never allow that fact to change their behavior.

Let me explain where I am coming from. In high school, I was the "Nice Guy". You all know what that means. If girls were asked what they thought of me, they would say (with genuine feeling, I believe), "Oh, he's a nice guy." This phrase of course was a death sentence to any hope of me ever having a date. Despite my lack of a girlfriend, I still had a lot of girl friends. I attribute this to the fact that I was so safe. I kept secrets, I was a good listener, I was nice, and I was totally nerdy and awkward and un-cool so even if I wanted to make a move on a girl, the girl would have nothing to fear because it would never work. Not that I would ever make a move, because I was a Nice Guy. I will explain this further in a later chapter, but it has to do with "The Code of the Nice Guy" that all Nice Guys live by. Anyway, since I was so harmless, girls thought I was the perfect guy friend to bring all of their dating questions and problems to. It usually went something like this:

First the girl would meet some absolutely gorgeous guy and fall madly in love with him. I don't want you to think this was an impetuous, spur of the moment type thing. In fact, sometimes it would take all of first period.

Which meant that I would hear about it in second period. I would tell her that I thought the guy was a Jerk, and that she should avoid him. I would give her reasons for my opinion, which she would ignore, and then she would proceed to date this guy. Things would be great at first. Then problems would start. The girl would come to me for advice. I would explain that it was because the guy was a Jerk, and she should dump him. "Yes, he's a Jerk," she would say, "but I love him!" She would then embark on a quest to change him, which would not work. Depending on the guy's goals and girls tolerance for abuse, the relationship would last anywhere from a week to several months. In the end, she would come to me heartbroken. Being a Nice Guy, I would never say, "I told you so," or "You're stupid. Next time listen to me." No, I would give her a shoulder to cry on as she described what a Jerk he was, and what qualities her perfect guy would have.

Those qualities, I would like to point out, are all of the qualities of the Nice Guy. So here I was with a girl who would never consider dating me because I am a Nice Guy, being told how she wishes that she could find a guy with those qualities. I could have given her the names of a dozen guys that were exactly what she said she wanted, and she would have laughed at the list, dismissing them all as "Nice Guys", and then proceeded to find another Jerk to date.

I am not the only Nice Guy that has this bitter

memory of high school. I have several friends from different states who had the exact same experience. That's why I say girls are stupid. They make a list of what they want. They see that there are two groups of guys that appear to have those qualities, "Cool Guys" and "Nice Guys." Nice Guys are boring, so girls date Cool Guys. Most Cool Guys turn out to be Jerks, but the girls stubbornly keep dating them, admitting that they actually have none of the qualities that they are looking for, and continuing to dismiss Nice Guys as just being "Nice Guys".

I say that that is the reason I think women are stupid, but there is another factor, as well. Women start off with all the advantages. They are the prize. They have something more precious than money or power. Money and power would have very little meaning to most men if there were no women. Women are the thing that men would give anything to have, and would do anything for. It would stand to reason, then, that women could set the rules, and make men do or give anything that women wanted. Women should have all the power. Rather than keeping the upper hand, however, they debase themselves, indulging in self-degradation and giving away their most precious possession.

One of my girl friends once asked me, after one of many bad experiences with a guy, why it was that all men wanted was sex. I had the perfect response, of course, about two weeks later. When she asked the question, my mind was totally blank, and I had nothing useful to say. But two weeks later, when she didn't care any more, I came up with the perfect answer.

Why is it that all guys want is sex? Because girls keep giving it to them.

Women are the most beautiful and wonderful creatures to ever grace the face of the earth. They are pretty much what every man wants. But they let men convince them that they are nothing special, that their bodies are not sacred, and that they are merely sex toys—so that is how they should act. Women get tricked into believing that if they want anything good in life, if they ever want to be loved, then they better act the way that men say they should. Otherwise, men won't want them, won't associate with them, and will never love them.

In fact, the exact opposite is true. By giving away their most precious virtues in the cheapest fashion, women lose all value to men. They become something that men would never respect. Men never give such women enough consideration or time to ever love them. Rather than being the fairy-tale princesses of priceless virtue that brave knights cross deserts and fight dragons for, they become cheap whores to be used for gratification, and dismissed afterwards as refuse.

Again, this may sound very harsh and hardly possible,

but it is true. Women don't know that this is how they are thought of because men disguise it. The way that men think of women is probably the greatest cover-up of all history. If you have trouble believing this, consider these questions:

Does pornography have anything to do with love?

Is pornography dying out, or is it a multi-billion dollar industry that spans the world?

Who spends the most money on pornography, men or women?

Does pornography engender respect towards women, or does it objectify them?

The truth is that women can choose how men think of them. If they make themselves a rare and precious treasure, they will be treated as such. If you want to be rescued by that knight, make yourself that difficult to obtain. If you are as available as a nickel in the gutter, men will never have to lift their minds out of the gutter to consider what you are really worth.

Chapter Three

Bear Bait or Bear Safe?

As a young teenager, I was very active in the Boy Scout program. As a result, I became an experienced camper. Part of that experience was having my food stolen by bears. It turns out that bears have quite the sweet tooth. Not only that, bears are pretty clever, and have figured out that where there are campers, there is candy. Many a camper has awoken to the sound of a bear rooting through the ice chest, or the sight of a bear sticking its head into the tent in search of candy, or even to the frightful experience of a bear licking chocolate residue off of their unwashed face.

This seems scary, but there were some very simple rules that made camping bear-able. First, never feed the bears. Invariably, the bears stomach is larger than your pockets, and you will run out of candy long before the bear's chocolate cravings are satisfied, which does not make for a very happy bear. There's nothing like an unhappy bear shaking you down for more candy. Two, don't leave food where it is accessible. We would put our food in thick metal boxes, or hang it in between two trees. Since bears can climb trees, you can't just hang it in the tree—you have to hang it between trees, and far enough between the trees that the bear can't jump out and grab it. Three, after denying the bear of your food, try not to look like food yourself. Bears are predators. Prey runs from predators. Prey is afraid of predators. If you act afraid or run, the bear will come to the logical conclusion that if you are afraid of it eating you, it must mean that you are something it wants to eat. Strangely enough, these three rules of bear safety can be applied to men.

RULE #1: DON'T FEED THE BEARS

Don't give the 'bears' a taste of anything that will whet an insatiable appetite for more. Odds are that he will end up wanting more than you are willing to give him. Men can be very persuasive, and will probably end up getting it out of you. The nice term for this is "getting played." The more accurate term is "being used." And it means that you lose. So what is it that you shouldn't be offering to the 'bears'? Kissing.

This is very important, so I'm going to say it again. NO KISSING!!!

There are a couple of other things that you should be wary of doing, such as holding hands or hugging, but kissing is one thing that you absolutely do not want to do. (Well, you probably do want to, because most of us do, but let's talk about why you don't want to more than you want to.) As I stated earlier, most men only want one thing—physical gratification. Their motivations are entirely selfish, purely hormonal, and rarely have anything to do with love. In the mildest of cases, the guy is looking for a kiss. In most cases, he wants sex. And kissing always comes before sex. (Granted, it is possible that you could bypass kissing, but we all know that realistically the only way that would ever happen is if you were born without lips, and he had had some sort of freak accident earlier that day involving superglue and lip balm.) So whether the guy is looking for kissing or looking for more than that, if you don't kiss him, he won't get what he is looking for, and he will move on.

A lot of guys actually have a set limit for the number of dates they will go on with a girl without having sex before they will give up on her and move on. The highest celibacy tolerance I have ever heard of in these men is three. If you haven't slept with them by date three, then you're history. For most of these Jerks, though, if you haven't kissed them by the end of date one, you will never see them again. Not kissing is the most powerful Jerk repellant known to woman. It is also how you become the player instead of the played. Let's consider a guy with a three-date limit.

Date one: Perhaps dinner and a movie. Cool. Worst-case scenario is, if he never calls you back, you got a free dinner and a movie. But we'll pretend that he is more persistent, and tries again.

Date two: This one is definitely going to be something a little more fun and interactive, so that he can exhibit how cool and desirable he is. If you dropped the right hints on your first date, maybe he'll take you to that play that you've been dying to see, or horseback riding, or something like that.

Date three: This could be one of two things—a last ditch effort, or a pathetic move to cut his losses. If it is the first, this date will be great, and will probably involve his place somehow. Maybe he'll cook you a dinner to eat by candlelight. Or, if he's not too handy in the kitchen, he might opt for a nice drive to a secluded scenic overlook where you can enjoy the stars. If he is cutting his losses, then you'll probably be back to just dinner and a movie. Either way, if you keep your cool, at the end of the date that Jerk is history, and you had three nights of free food and entertainment.

You might feel that there is something wrong to this approach. After all, wouldn't playing the player make you as bad as the player? It would, if your entire motivation was to get free stuff from guys by deceiving them. But if you are simply following the 'no kissing' rule, there is no deception. Tell them up front what your rules are. If they still want to try, that's up to them. Enjoy the free food.

So, 'No Kissing' is a great way to ensure Jerks won't ask you out again, but what about the guys that aren't Jerks? Will it discourage the Nice Guys as well? I will answer this in depth later on when I talk about Nice Guys. For now, here is the short answer: No. If the guy really cares about you, and is interested in you for who you are, not what he can get out of you, he will keep asking you out. It may seem that you are scaring away Nice Guys by not kissing them, but I can guarantee you that you aren't. All you are getting rid of is Jerks acting nice to get you off guard. You might consider the 'No Kissing' rule as a sort of litmus test for determining if a guy has potential, or if he's just a Jerk. Believe me, the Jerks will go, and the Nice Guys will stay. In fact, they will be more likely to stay when they see that you respect yourself, and that you're not just another baton in a sex-relay.

The difficult part is when you have an actual relationship (meaning that you relate well with each other, not just that you have eaten more than three meals together or seen three movies together) and you want to kiss each other because you really do love each other. I am not going to tell you that you shouldn't kiss until you're married. I have no moral objection to kissing. But I will give you one warning: You're relationship better be founded on something more meaningful and exciting than kissing, or kissing will be the flood that washes away everything that you had. You will quickly find that all he wants to do is kiss, even if he is a 'Nice Guy', because even Nice Guys produce testosterone. And as I said earlier, kissing is just a stepping-stone to ultimate intimacy. If you proceed down that road too quickly, without adequately establishing your route and goals along the way, you will get lost, and lose all that you had, and all that you might have had. I have seen more than a few friends, guys and girls, ruin great relationships—relationships that had 'happily ever after' potential—by getting too physical, too soon.

So I say play it safe—NO KISSING! Yes, that will take self-control, but everything truly good in life comes at the expense of self-discipline. Anything cheaper will not bring lasting happiness. If you are looking for a good man, who will love and respect you, who will commit to a relationship of complete fidelity, you have to be a woman who is worth that commitment. You both have to be committed to that relationship before you have even found it. There are some who may stumble upon such a relationship without such commitment, but I believe it is only by the occasional coincidence, and usually only after a fair amount of heartbreak preceding it.

I am trying to give you a better and less painful method of finding true love.

Besides, kissing just increases your chance of catching the flu.

RULE #2: HIDE YOUR FOOD FROM THE BEARS

Leaving your food out in the open is the surest way to invite unwanted wildlife into your camp. Obviously, you can't camp without food, so you have to have it somewhere, but you don't want to leave it out as an open invitation to anything with four legs, a nose and a mouth. Lock it up, hide it high out of reach, put it in a scent-proof bag—do something with it to make it less of a temptation to the bears. Likewise, when there is a hungry man on the prowl, you should consider carefully how you package yourself.

In the meat market of dating, there are certain cuts of meat that especially appeal to the male appetite—thighs, breasts, buttocks, and midriff. Hide them.

I understand that women want to look good. Everyone wants to be attractive. But what is it that you are trying to attract? What is it that you want men to think about you? Do you want them to think about you, or do you want them to think about sex? The reason that short skirts and tank tops are sexy is because they make men think about sex. That's why men like women to dress that way. When a man sprains his neck to get a second look at a bikini clad babe on the beach, it's not because he is wondering if he could engage her in a stimulating debate on current political issues. He is thinking, "I want to have sex with that!" Notice the 'that', because it's important. In his most carnal desires, women are not people, they are just objects.

So how do you promote yourself as a person rather than an object? It's all in how you dress. If you want to be considered as a person, you need to dress in a way that emphasizes you as a whole, not you as individual parts. There are certain things that are extremely sexually stimulating to a man visually. At the top of that list are a woman's breasts. If any portion of your breasts are highly accentuated or showing, that is what a man is going to concentrate on. Women do not understand the hypnotic power that their breasts have over men. Remember the opening scene of Bay Watch, where the various well-endowed lifeguards are running down the beach in slow motion, bouncing like a bra full of jell-o? Men could sit and watch that all day long. If TiVo had been invented back then, no man would have ever made it past the opening credits. Point is, men love to stare at women's breasts, so if you ever want a man to notice what color your eyes are, you have to give him a reason to look higher than your chest.

Running a close second is the buttocks. Hopefully you're not walking around mooning the world, but an unreasonably tight skirt or pair of jeans will have nearly the same affect. Next on the list, and closely related anatomically, are the thighs. Short skirts and short shorts will really get men fantasizing. Last of all is a good looking tummy. Naked midriffs are a killer if they look good.

You have probably noticed that all of the specific regions I have noted happen to be the portions of the body that trendy clothing fails to cover. That's a problem, I know. However, I also know girls that have managed to still dress attractively, stylishly, and less-nakedly all at the same time. It takes effort, but it is possible. You have to decide what it is you want guys to be thinking when they look at you. Do you want them to see you as only a pair of boobs? Do you want every man in the grocery store to be imagining how great it would be to get you naked? Whether you are a real person or a sexual fantasy is up to you.

It is possible to dress attractively without being provocative. I'm not going to go into detail on specific styles and outfits, because I can barely make my own clothes match. However, I want to point out some things that men do find attractive without causing them to think about sex. A good smile is incredibly attractive. So are pretty eyes, nice hair, and good posture. (Yeah, I know I sounded like your mother on that last one, but it's true.) Cultivate those aspects of your beauty, and dress in a way that will not attract too much attention away from them. Those are the things that bring you out as a person. They are things that make a man curious about your personality, and add to who you are intellectually. While a Nice Guy is as stimulated by a great pair of legs in a short skirt as the next guy, what he is really looking for is a smile that expresses real enjoyment of life, and a posture that is confident and self-assured. A woman that can draw attention without flaunting her body is a woman worth getting to know.

RULE #3: DON'T LOOK LIKE FOOD

If you are getting bored, then my brief exposition on this rule should come as a relief. Put simply, it is this: If a guy hears how you were 'played', he will see you as an easy target, because guys know that girls rarely learn from their mistakes. In other words, if you tell a guy that you aren't interested in anything more than a friend because you just got out of a relationship where you got used by a real Jerk, you are just painting a big red target on yourself for any Jerk in earshot. One of the easiest and most common moves in the 'Players Guide to Playing Girls" is for the player to act like the supportive-but-harmless nice guy who is there just to be a friend. This is why so many girls immediately go from bad relationship to bad relationship.

Also, complaining about failed relationships is not only unattractive, but if there is a Nice Guy interested in you, and you tell him that you hate men and don't want to date, he will respect that and back off, possibly for good. So, lament the evils of men all you want with other girls, but keep your failed relationships as quiet as possible when around guys.

RULE #4: THE WILDLIFE IS WILD

In other words, bears, cougars, wolves and skunks do not make good pets. They are wild animals, and that nature can't be changed. Even tigers that are raised by humans from birth can still be unpredictably dangerous predators. That is their nature. Women make the tremendous fallacy of believing that they can change men. It is because of this foible in their nature that they will hang onto a Jerk for as long as they can, enduring neglect, disrespect, and sometimes abuse, until *he* finally gets tired of *her* and moves on. They love him, and think they can change him.

I don't want to sound like I've lost all faith in humanity. I truly believe that any person can change for the better. If I didn't believe people could change, I wouldn't be writing this. I also believe it is possible to love a person who is bad, and who treats you poorly. However, I believe there is a right way and a wrong way to help that person change. Think of it this way:

Pretend you have a dog that you are trying to teach not to beg. Every time he begs, you scold him, and then give him a scrap of meat or a dog biscuit. Do you think he will ever stop begging? No. Why? Because he doesn't have to change his behavior in order to get what he wants. You give it to him no matter what. If you are in love with a Jerk, and you want him to change, you have to explain the rules to him, and then stick by those rules. If he can have you and still be a Jerk, odds are that he will always be a Jerk. If he knows that he has to change in order to be with you, he will have a lot more incentive to change. If he doesn't change, you are better off without him.

It *is* possible to love more than one person. Just because two people love each other doesn't mean that their relationship will work out. It takes more than love, and it could be that there is someone else that each of them could love, with whom they would be more compatible and have a better relationship.

I know that logic flies in the face of every romantic movie ever made, but it is true. Don't sell yourself short. Don't go into a relationship thinking that you can change a man's entire nature. You will fail, and he will make you miserable. Leave the bears in the woods, and take home a puppy that is loving and faithful.

Chapter Four

The Problem with Nice Guys

In a perfect world, there would be perfect guys. In this world, there are only guys who you don't know well enough yet to see their flaws. And 98.7% of them are Jerks. But don't give up all hope yet. There are nice guys out there. You just have to realize that they are not perfect.

One of the most frequent questions I am asked as a Nice Guy is this: Why are Nice Guys always so weird? I consider this a perfectly valid question. Unfortunately, it is not a question with an easy answer. And it only gets harder. How do you spot a Nice Guy? How do you tell the difference between a Nice Guy and a Jerk without getting hurt first? Why don't Nice Guys ever make a move to rescue the girl from the Jerks? These are hard questions.

The easy answer is, "I don't know." But that would make for a short and somewhat disappointing book, so I will try to do better. Please bear with me, as Nice Guys are very elusive individuals, and finding them is much like finding water in the desert. You have to ignore the tempting mirages, know what you're looking for, and be ready to dig a little below the surface of what appears to be plain, dry sand.

Let's start with what exactly it is you're looking for. What are the characteristics of a Nice Guy? What is the best way to spot one? As I've thought about it (and I've thought about it a lot—it's taken me two years to get from chapter three to chapter four), the most defining characteristic of a Nice Guy is that he is *nice*. Profound, isn't it?

Seriously, though, that is what makes the difference. Nice Guys are nice to everyone. They are kind and respectful to their mothers. They are helpful to strangers. They don't discriminate against the ugly or obnoxious or unpopular. They are loving towards their brothers and sisters. When a Nice Guy treats you with kindness and respect, it's not because you're different, it's just because he treats everyone that way.

Jerks, on the other hand, tend to be Jerks (shocking, isn't it?). They are nice to people only when they think they can get something in return. They can be respectful to their boss when they need a raise, or loving to their mother when they need a big favor, or nice to a nerd when they need help on their homework. But as a rule, they are selfish, and are only nice when it works out to their advantage.

A lot of women are easily fooled, and only notice that

their boyfriend is nice to them. They fail to catch the fact that he is mean to everyone else. I had a friend that fell into this trap. She thought her boyfriend was the greatest guy ever. What she couldn't see was that he had no respect for his family, and treated her family like dirt, as well. He was rude to cashiers, made fun of other people, and cut in line. Friends and family tried to warn her that he was trouble, but she said that they "just didn't understand him", that "she was changing him", and that "he treated her well."

As time went on, and as she committed more to the relationship, he didn't treat her as well. He became more demanding, got angry at her, made fun of her, and only let them do the things he wanted to do. In other words, once he got what he wanted, he treated her just like he treated everyone else.

If every Jerk were like the one above, they would be fairly easy to spot. If you are on a date, and he verbally abuses the waitress, you know exactly what sort of man he is. Unfortunately, the worst ones are smoother than that, and not as easy to spot. They are not only nice to you, they are nice to everyone—as long as you are around. They may even go so far as to be nice around the people they know talk to you on a regular basis. This makes things a lot more difficult.

So how can you know when the kindness is just a mirage? First, listen to the advice of people around you. If everyone around you thinks the guy is a Jerk, odds are that he is. Second, don't give him anything in return. Once he realizes that his effort to deceive you isn't getting him anywhere, he'll show himself to be the Jerk he really is.

While the Jerks may stand in line to get your attention, the best way to find a Nice Guy is to be looking for one. Observe the guys around you. If there is one that is a Jerk everyday until the day he talks to you, and then all of the sudden he's the sweetest thing, don't waste your time. However, if you notice a guy that is nice to everyone day after day, take a chance and go talk to him. Maybe there won't be a romantic flame, and maybe you aren't attracted to him at all, but it never hurts to be friends with a Nice Guy. You can learn what a genuinely nice guy is really like, so you can spot them easier in the future. You'll have someone you can trust when he gives you advice about other guys. Best of all, you'll learn what it's like to have a guy care about you and respect you for who you are, not what he hopes you'll give him. Like water in the desert, such friendships are an oasis of comfort among life's vast expanses of pretense and self-interest.

Unfortunately, most Nice Guys aren't as obvious or inviting as an oasis. In fact, like most water in the desert, Nice Guys usually don't appear to be worth a second glance. In the desert, water hides beneath the sand, or inside strange looking plants. In life, Nice Guys are weird.

Actually, Nice Guys are just different. I would like to

take a moment to eliminate a stereotype. Not all nice guys are weird, and not all weird guys are nice. I have known very nice guys who played football, dressed in style, and were well liked by everyone. I have also known many

nerds (and other assorted weirdo's) that had just as dirty of minds as the next guy, but lacked the necessary charm needed to act on their dirty fantasies. It is important to realize that I am not advocating that every girl should trade "tall, dark and handsome" for "pale, awkward and pimply." Indiscriminately dating the strange and introverted will only lead to a whole new set of problems, like stalkers.

This is not to say that Nice Guys are not different, and to some of us, even a little weird. I believe there is a very good reason for this, however. Another common characteristic of Nice Guys is that they don't spend a lot of time worrying about what the rest of the world thinks of them. The majority of us are largely preoccupied with making sure that our every action and outfit is socially acceptable. We wear what society tells us is stylish, and we do what we think other people will think is cool. Nice Guys, on the other hand, lead lives that are a little less shallow.

Consider my brother, for instance. He's fascinated by magnets. He has a collection that includes hundreds of magnets, big and small, weak and powerful. Of course, his favorites are the really strong ones. He carries these magnets around with him, and plays with them whenever he sees something interesting he can try with them. To a lot of people, this is very disturbing. It's not normal to play with magnets, or even carry them around with you for that matter. You could try to explain this to him, but he wouldn't care. He does what he enjoys, not what other people think he should enjoy.

I was also a little weird in high school. I had tape on my glasses because we didn't have the money to buy me new ones right away. I never wore shorts because I hated getting my legs scraped up every time I took a short cut or had a bike wreck. And I carried a briefcase.

Now, before you judge me, let me explain all of the advantages of a briefcase. Briefcases are longer and skinnier than backpacks, so they fit more conveniently in the aisle between desks. Mine had a lock, so people couldn't steal my homework. A briefcase makes a great improvised desk for writing on, or a table for eating lunch. They have lots of pockets for filing papers and keeping pens, pencils, paperclips, highlighters, calculators, staplers, staples, erasers, pocket dictionaries, stick-it notes, rubber bands, rulers, protractors, and spare batteries organized. When you get caught in the rain, you can use a briefcase as an umbrella, and it still keeps all of your papers dry. And in the event of a water landing, your briefcase may be used as a flotation device.

Okay, I never actually tested that last one, but the point is that a briefcase is a very useful thing, and I thought it was way better than a backpack, so I used one at school. Not surprisingly, other people did not think that it was very cool. I endured a lot of teasing over my beloved briefcase, and on several occasions proved that I could—without dropping said briefcase—outrun anyone who might want to harm me or it. I knew that carrying a briefcase made me a nerd (or at least *nerdier*), and that I probably wasn't going to win any popularity contests while I had it. But I didn't care. I liked it, and it was practical, so I kept it.

Carrying the briefcase did not change who I was. Had I left it home and carried a backpack I would have still acted the same and treated other people the same. The only difference between me and the guys that everyone thought were cool was my briefcase…and the tape on my glasses…and the fact I was shy…and—alright, so there were a lot of things that made me un-cool, but they were very superficial. The biggest problem with Nice Guys is that they are not superficial, but they live in a world that places great value in superficial things. Nice Guys value beliefs, interests, friendships, trust, respect, and understanding. That's why Nice Guys are nice. They care about who people really are—their hopes and dreams, abilities and potential—not about how they dress, what they look like, where they shop, or how they talk.

Because Nice Guys invest their time in worrying about what matters, they are not as well versed or adept in the shallow conventions of society. As a result, they are different. They don't act like everyone else. They act like themselves. And they won't treat you like everyone else treats you. They'll treat you like they treat everyone else.

Chapter Five

The Nice Guy: A Knight in Shining Armor Who Will Never Rescue You

Once upon a time there was a young and beautiful princess. She was the daughter of the king of all the land. That is why she was a princess. You can only be a princess if your father is the king. This princess had all of the charms that a princess should have. Namely, she was beautiful and rich.

The princess could have anything she wanted, and she was the object of every man's dreams, noble and poor alike. But despite having everything a girl could dream of, she longed for more. She wanted excitement.

Just outside of her father's kingdom, in the wild and dangerous forest, there lived a dragon. The dragon never bothered the kingdom, because he wasn't very interested in civilization and rules. He much preferred eating the cute little forest animals.

One day the princess, in search of adventure, decided it would be fun to go talk to the dangerous dragon. Her parents warned her against it, as did her teachers and other responsible civic leaders, but she ignored them. There was something very romantic about the thought of being almost killed by a dragon, and then possibly being rescued by a knight.

Of course there were knights in the kingdom. There was one in particular whom the king really liked. He was bright and well mannered, and worked hard to take care of his serfs. He found the practice of dragon slaying to be very impractical, however, so the princess thought him to be somewhat boring. The knight, of course, thought the princess was being stupid—dragons are very dangerous, after all—but he knew that she wouldn't listen to him, and

he also knew the dragon would be very likely to kill him, or at least embarrass him very badly, if he tried to interfere.

At first, everything went great between the princess and the dragon. She visited him day after day, until one day the dragon burned her to a crisp and ate her.

The knight, who was quite worried about her, decided at that point that he would be better off not rescuing her, seeing how she was already devoured.

The End

The moral of this story is the subject of this chapter, and the answer to a question that I am often asked: Why don't Nice Guys make a move to rescue the girls from all of the Jerks?

This question is often posed as an accusation from girls who just got out of a bad relationship with a Jerk. They'll be complaining about how there are no nice guys, to which I'll argue that there *are* nice guys—it's just that they (the girls) have been doing all of the wrong things. Of course, the girls disagree, but eventually I get them to see the error of their ways. Then, rather than admitting that they could make some changes to their own behavior to solve the problem, they try to lay it back at the feet of Nice Guys by saying that their (the girls') dating woes are the fault of Nice Guys for not asking the poor girls out. So if you are a woman reading this, and you are feeling that same hostility toward Nice Guys, this chapter is for you.

The first important point that I would like to make is this: the world is not kind to Nice Guys. It takes a lot of courage and resolve to be a Nice Guy. I know from experience that Nice Guys are not usually the most popular people, especially among other men. A good lesson on how males live can be learned from watching the apes at the zoo for about half an hour. There you'll see that there is one ape that is in charge. He is usually larger than the other males, and as you watch him, you'll probably notice that he is a bit of a bully. Whatever he wants, he gets, because he's the biggest and the toughest. The other males spend a lot of time also trying to act tough to impress each other, and catch the eye of the females. The quiet apes mostly get their food stolen, and get ignored by the females.

Adolescent males, much like apes, spend a lot of time pounding their chests and yelling, so to speak. Male dominance among humans is established by macho behavior, tough talk, nice cars, humor, insults, and the occasional fistfight. As much as women like to deride men for the hairy, uncultured apes that they are, women are attracted to the tough guys, just like their lady-ape counterparts.

What does this mean for Nice Guys? First of all, it means that they are almost always at the bottom of the pecking order. It's not because they aren't tough, or because they can't think of witty insults, or because they couldn't afford a nice car. It's because they don't choose to engage in such primitive behavior. They believe that real men aren't apes. As a result, they don't let themselves get provoked into fights, and they avoid conflict as much as possible. Thus they look weak. When insulted, they don't dirty themselves by scooping a reply out of the gutter, and so they remain silent as others laugh at them. While their peers are working to pay for a nice car, they are saving their money for college and a future, so they don't have the nicest ride. Because of all this, most of them will experience many years of being made fun of and rejected.

All of this usually happens before guys have even finished puberty, so that by the time Nice Guys might be interested in talking to girls, they are already accustomed to approaching people with caution. This timid behavior often makes them look weak, which usually doesn't score big points with the ladies. Also, it means that the Jerks beat them to all of the girls. All of this results in the mess that is all around us.

One of the most frustrating things is that parents,

who are typically older and more mature, recognize Nice Guys for the great catch that they are, and constantly point them out to their daughters. I was very popular with parents when I was in high school. I was just a geek to all of my classmates. Like the knight in the previous story, all of the qualities that make Nice Guys stand out to the parents—good manners, academic success, responsibility, solid goals—are exactly the same qualities that make them boring to everyone their age.

Anyway, the whole system is very confusing to Nice Guys. They spend their lives pursuing what they feel are noble goals. Adults, books, movies, and girls tell them that the qualities they possess are what women are really looking for, but at every turn they are passed up for some Jerk that has none of those qualities. And it gets worse.

As Nice Guys are working hard to develop all of the qualities on women's wish lists, the Jerks are getting in lots of practice at abusing the system. This is how they become players. A player is more than just a Jerk. A player is a Jerk that is very good at playing the game, and at playing women. Players learn that what women say they want is not what women are most strongly attracted to. Players know exactly what it is that women will fall for, and that's what they give them.

Now we have set the stage for a drama, and in this case, a tragedy. Like the princess in our story, there is a girl searching for love and companionship who gets distracted by the promise of mystery and excitement. Like the dragon, the player maintains a façade of friendliness and charm at the beginning of the relationship. Soon the girl is mesmerized by his personality and slave to his every strategy, though she never realizes it. From a distance the Nice Guy sees it all. He knows the player is just a Jerk, and he knows that the girl deserves better than that. He definitely feels that the way she is being used is wrong, and that the way she'll be hurt is truly sad. It would seem the perfect time for our hero to ride in from the side and rescue the poor girl, right?

Wrong. Like the knight who didn't know how to fight dragons, the Nice Guy knows that he is way out of his league trying to take on a player. He doesn't know anything about how to brandish wit, parry an insult, or use charm alone to disarm a person. He is not cocky enough to walk like he's god's-gift-to-women. The Nice Guy is already behind in the game, and if he were to match himself against a player, he'd just get burned, and be thoroughly humiliated. This, of course, would only make the player even more attractive, and force the Nice Guy to accept permanent defeat.

Instead, the Nice Guy employs a different, more subtle strategy. It is one that is equally doomed to failure, but ultimately less painful for him. He closes his eyes and wishes *really* hard that the girl would quit being so stupid.

All right, he doesn't do that, exactly. What he really

does is try to get the girl to notice him by being in the same general area as her (the desk next to her if he's brave; on the same planet if he's really shy) and then acting like himself. Of course, the girl *never* notices him, which is why women are always complaining that there are no nice guys. In the end, he contemplates committing suicide—not literally, just in the sense of actually talking to the girl or confronting her boyfriend. Before he can muster up the courage and devise a proper plan, the girl usually succumbs to the Jerk's illicit tactics, becoming yet another successful conquest.

This is the unpleasant part of our story where the dragon devours the princess. In the story, the knight gives up on rescuing her after she has already been eaten. Unfortunately, you'll find that in real life it goes much the same way. The Nice Guy will cease his efforts to get the girl's attention the moment he thinks she has had sex with the Jerk. I know that sounds very harsh, and this is a sensitive subject that makes a lot of women mad. I hope that I can explain it well.

Here's the problem. As I stated before, it's not easy being a Nice Guy. It would be much easier for them to give in to the primitive lusts and emotions associated with being a man, and live life selfishly, than to hold themselves to a higher standard of discipline and humanity. In general, people don't make such sacrifices unless they have faith in some greater good. In this case, Nice Guys believe that there is a finer happiness and a more noble existence than living as animals. They believe that humans are more capable of love, kindness, trust, and joy than the other inhabitants of earth. They have faith that by sacrificing the instant gratification that comes from pursuing shallow and selfish ambitions they can achieve a more lasting happiness and the satisfaction of fulfilling their greatest potential. They are also searching for someone who shares that belief, and has made the same sacrifices in order to find true love and happiness.

A girl who casually surrenders her most valuable virtues is not the woman that a Nice Guy is waiting for.

This does not mean that all hope is lost if you have given up your virginity. Sometimes a discussion of this subject will lead someone to use the phrase "used goods" to describe such women. I want to make it clear that Nice Guys do not think that way.

First of all, women are not "goods." A woman is a person, not a product intended for personal recreation. Second, "used" is a permanent state, irreversible, never to be new again. While people cannot retrace the events that led to certain mistakes, they can learn from those mistakes, and become better. While a Nice Guy would love to meet a woman that has always respected herself enough to guard her virtue, that is not necessarily what he is looking for. In fact, there are Nice Guys out there that have made the same mistakes. What a Nice Guy is really looking for is a woman that has that respect for herself *now*. He wants her to have the same hope of true love, and the same faith in the higher dignity of humankind. He is looking for a woman that believes in those same principles enough that she now treats herself and others as sacrosanct.

So in the end, while a Nice Guy wishes with all of his might that he had the ability to rescue all of the girls from all of the Jerks and save them all of the heartache, he knows that what he is really hoping to find is that special woman who does not need rescued, because she knows that she is a princess, and too precious to be fooling around with dragons.

Chapter Six

Before You Buy That "Fixer-Upper"

The most burning question on Nice Guys' minds is this: Why do girls always go for the Jerks? Female behavior is a continual source of puzzlement and discouragement for them. Strangely enough, I have heard many women ask the same question, so apparently they are just as confused and concerned about their own behavior. I decided to do a little research into the matter and see if I could come up with a plausible hypothesis.

My exhaustive research was comprised of two important parts. First, I thought really hard to come up with my own answer. Second, I asked all of the girls I knew who were dating Jerks *why* they were dating such Jerks. This comprehensive study resulted in two possible explanations, and a few angry women.

The first explanation is the result of my own consideration of the matter. My observation has been that girls don't always start out dating a Jerk thinking that he is a Nice Guy.

Often, the girl is well aware of the fact that he is a Jerk, and has voiced her opinion on it several times. I can't count the number of times I have seen a girl absolutely despise some guy because he is a Jerk—watched them fight and insult each other—then seen them making out behind the gym. I saw it in high school. I saw it in college. I saw it in the army. I've seen it on those stupid reality dating shows. And I am always amazed at how quickly girls can lower their standards in order to get swept off their feet by some Jerk.

Consider the example of a guy and girl I knew in the army. The guy, who we will call Sam, was a complete Jerk. No one, man or woman, liked him. He was conceited, arrogant, vulgar, lazy, and rude. I met Sam the first night at basic training, and got to know him well (much to my dismay) over the next ten weeks. We were at an all-male boot camp, so most of the guys, including Sam, were very free with their opinions on sex and women. One night, just a few days before graduation, Sam and I had KP duty together, which is where we had to wash all of the dishes and clean the chow hall. Naturally, our excitement over leaving boot camp soon was a topic of conversation. Both of us were going into the same military job, so we would both be leaving for Ft. Sam Houston after graduation.

Sam asked me, "So, are you ready to go be a man-whore?" I tried to ignore the question, but he persisted, so I asked him what he was talking about. He told me that rumor had it that Ft. Sam was the only army base that had more women than men. Unlike other military posts, where you were lucky to get a girlfriend so you had to treat her well to keep her from being stolen by some other soldier, Ft. Sam had an overabundance of women, so you could get what you wanted, and move on. His plan was to try and get with at least two new girls every weekend. I told him he was a sick pervert, and did my best to ignore him the rest of the evening.

Two weeks later, we were in Texas. Ft. Sam turned out not to have the hundred girls for every guy that legend said it did, but it did have a better ratio than boot camp. Unfortunately for Sam, we had three weeks of training before we were allowed to leave the base for the weekend. During this time we got to know all of the other soldiers training there with us, and they all came to hate Sam. Sam let everyone know that he was the smartest one there. Sam never did his share of the duties. Sam was annoying. Among those who despised him was a female soldier whom we will call Anne. Anne and I became friends, so when Sam first made an attempt at her, she told me all about it.

Her opinion was that Sam was despicable and disgusting, and she wanted nothing to do with him. This opinion only grew firmer as he built a reputation as the guy that would get any girl drunk in order to get her to have sex with him. Apparently, that was the only strategy that worked for him.

Unfortunately for Anne, her girl friends were friends with the only guys that let Sam hang out with them, so she spent the first half dozen free weekends forced to hang out in close proximity to Sam. She never stopped complaining about him. Then one weekend she had sex with him.

When I heard about it, I was shocked—and slightly sickened. I couldn't understand how a girl that was so well aware of what a Jerk Sam was, and so opposed to how he treated women, could so quickly lose all sense of self worth and do something so stupid. Now I have a theory.

My theory is this: The most important thing is that the girl feels some sort of strong emotion about a guy. Once she feels a strong emotion towards him, even if that emotion is hatred or disgust, the guy can use the fact that women are very confused about their emotions to trick her into thinking that she likes him.

A woman's feelings on a Nice Guy can be summed up in one phrase: "Oh, he's a nice guy, I guess." There is very little *real* feeling there. The guy is not the focus of an intense opinion or fierce emotion. Rather, he is the object of unremarkable apathy. She is largely indifferent to him. Even if he were to make a good impression, it would be of little importance, because he isn't important. It's not that girls don't think highly of Nice Guys, they just don't think about Nice Guys much at all.

A guy that is a real Jerk, on the other hand, can

become a skilled player. He knows that the passionate abhorrence a girl feels toward him is what puts him in the game. Maybe she doesn't like him, but at least she thinks about him, and has made room within her emotions for him. From there it's just a matter of playing her right. A slick player will manipulate her emotions and fool her into thinking that she is actually incredibly attracted to him. It's tricky, but he only needs to maintain the illusion long enough to get what he wants.

If you do not agree with that explanation of the universe as we know it, then consider this second theory, which was given to me by a woman. It's very simple: Women like projects. Women like to create, grow, design, and remodel things. They rearrange furniture, plant gardens, redecorate homes, and coordinate outfits. Women, in general, like to make the world around them better. I know this sounds very sexist, but like I said, this was first explained to me by a woman.

Following this line of reason, we find ourselves at the ultimate project: A wild, unrefined, raw man. He's handsome, he's fun, he's exciting, he's…a Jerk. He's disloyal, deceitful, disrespectful, demanding, and egocentric. But if she can only change him, he'll be Mr. Perfect, and she'll be his Mrs. Perfect. So she takes him on as a fun project.

The only problem is this: He's not a project. He's a player. He's taking advantage of her. He knows that he doesn't ever actually have to change; he only has to keep her hoping that he will change. As long as he can keep that dream alive, she will stick with him. It is the beginning of a very bad relationship.

On the girl's side of it, she gives him everything. She loves him, she serves him, and she does everything she can to please him. She invests her heart and soul into trying to make him see that she is the one. She knows that if she can just get him to realize that she will always be there to make him happy, then he will change his philandering ways. She believes that he doesn't mean to hurt her, and that if she keeps forgiving him and loving him, that one day he'll change. After all, it only takes 110 minutes for a man to come around in the movies.

On the guy's side of things, it's a great gig. He gets a girl that treats him like he's king. Her willing servitude meets his every need and desire, and makes him feel like he's important and powerful. He doesn't have to please her or respect her. All he has to do is make empty promises, and offer the occasional sweet gesture. He has no intention of changing. He takes everything she has to give and gives little, if anything, in return. Not only that, it feeds his selfish ego, and he begins wanting more than she can offer, so he uses other women at the same time. He doesn't even think of it as cheating, because he never felt any loyalty to the first woman. She is an object to him. He thinks of her as toy, a condiment for his pleasure, and a trophy to show off.

Women think that they can change this. They believe that they can modify men's behavior. The problem, however, is not that these men behave like Jerks. The problem is that deep down inside they really *are* Jerks.

While I was growing up, I learned proper table manners, and tried to use them, because I am, by nature, a polite person. That is part of being a Nice Guy. At the age of nineteen, I moved to Hong Kong for two years. By American standards, Chinese table manners are nonexistent. They talk with their mouth full, spit the bones out on the table, eat directly from the serving dishes in the middle of the table, and burp out loud at the end of the meal. However, the Chinese aren't lacking manners, they just have different rules. Some things that Americans do would be considered rude to them, such as not keeping both hands on the table during the meal. In America, it is polite to keep one hand in your lap. In China, that is a strange and rude behavior. Being a polite person, I quickly adopted these new rules of etiquette, and I have to admit that I kind of enjoyed them. When I returned to the U.S., I resumed the use of proper American table manners.

I have friends now that are from China. Sometimes they do things that Americans find very rude, but it is only because they are still trying to learn all of the customs. As soon as they learn the proper manners, they use them, because they also value being polite.

On the other hand, I know people who have been taught politeness all of their life, but are still unmannered and rude. When they belch out loud in a restaurant, it's not because they are ignorant, it's because they don't care. They are just plain rude.

My point is this: It is nearly impossible to change the fundamental nature of a person. If their actions are a reflection of their nature, then you can't modify their behavior. If they are rude, they will act rude, and you can't teach them better. If they are a Jerk, they will act like a Jerk, with little possibility of ever changing.

Think of it like an old house that is in poor repair—a real "fixer-upper." Some houses just need a few coats of paint, work on the roof, and some new carpet to return them to their original value. Others, however, have cracked foundations, rotted support beams, asbestos insulation, and are in a bad neighborhood. They might even still look great, but are worthless, and probably dangerous to live in. Unlike the first house, which was a little rough to look at but structurally sound, this house is rotten to the very core, and virtually impossible to fix.

So for all you women who are looking for a good project, I would like to make a suggestion. Avoid that second kind of house. Yes there are men that are your "dream house" on the outside—stylish, exciting, funny, and mysterious—but they are rotten and dangerous

when it comes to their actual character, and YOU CAN'T FIX THEM!

Instead, consider the Nice Guy that is a little aloof, perhaps awkward, and doesn't do the most exciting things for fun. On the outside, he is not the most attractive person, but on the inside, he is Mr. Wonderful. Make *him* your project. Be his friend, help him learn how to socialize and have fun, and teach him how to dress attractively. You can coach him on what women think is romantic, how to be exciting, and how to act more confident.

You don't have to date him or fall in love with him, just be a friend, and follow all the rules that I outlined earlier. You might be surprised what happens. While he is just another unremarkable, unattractive Nice Guy now, with a little help from a skilled coach (that's you, girls), he might end up being the next "Johnny Angel." It might take a little time and a lot of work, but at least you won't be used and abused in the process, which is what happens to women who hold out hope that their Jerk boyfriend will suddenly change.

Ultimately, if your strategy is to kiss a lot of frogs with the impossible hope that they will turn into a prince, you will only end up with disappointment and warts. If you want a prince, it is far better to start looking among the guys that treat you like a princess.

Chapter Seven

A Case Study

Some of you reading this right now are probably skeptical. You're thinking to yourselves, "Why would we believe this guy? He's just one person with a bitter view of the world. And did he really carry a briefcase in high school?!! What a doofus! He probably got beat up all the time, and *that's* why he hates guys."

Those are some excellent points, and I would like to take some time to respond to them. First, I really did carry a briefcase for the first two years of high school, and I never got beat up. (Coincidentally, those were the same two years that I lettered in Track)

Second, I was, in fact, a total doofus. Unlike carrying the briefcase, being a doofus lasted for all four years of high school, as well as for some years before and after.

Third, I *am* just one person, and most of the viewpoints and proof presented thus far have been from my own personal experience. If I were the only one with these arguments, there would be considerable reason for skepticism. Unfortunately, there is an overabundance of evidence in the world that what I say is true. Men taking advantage of women has been the larger part of the history of human civilization.

I recently read an excellent article written by Janet Reitman that vividly illustrates the point I have been trying to make. The article explores the culture of sex and relationships at a prestigious university campus. Being a competitive university, the students who attend are talented and intelligent. The article focuses on the thoughts and feelings of several of the female students. Janet Reitman describes the girls she interviewed as "formidable young women"[1] who earned straight A's in high school and played one or more sports. All of the girls were popular, and all of them were very stylish.

The women at this university are people that have great potential. They sound like the type of girl that every guy would dream of meeting, and with whom only an incredibly great guy would be worthy of being in a relationship. They work hard to be that type of woman. Some people worry that they work too hard. The article explains that in 2003, the university conducted a study on the social views and concerns of their female students. Many of those students said that they had to put tremendous effort into maintaining an illusion of "effortless perfection"[2]—

excelling academically while also being perfect physically. The girls felt pressured to get good grades, prestigious internships, have perfect skin and hair, stylish clothes, and a size-four feminine physique.

One of the girls admitted that there is a certain standard that she and her friends feel a need to live up to—being intelligent, scholarly, ambitious and purposeful as well as being cute, fashionable, devoted to working out, and fun.

At first glance, this really isn't that surprising. At a prestigious university one would expect that there would be a lot of intelligent and gorgeous guys and girls with bright futures, and that there would be a lot of pressure on each gender to be their best in order to impress each other. But here's the twist. The article goes on to explain that the guys at the university don't feel the same pressure to be perfect in order to impress the girls. The women who were interviewed said that the guys were always playing video games or just hanging out. They felt it was unfair that the guys could take it easy, while they were working so much harder—spending hours at the gym, eating fish, etc.—just to impress the guys.

It would seem that the women—beautiful, intelligent, talented, and motivated as they are—should be calling all of shots when it came to relationships. However, this is not the case. All of the pressure to be perfect falls very lop-sidedly upon the women, which is something that worries many of the professors at the university. They feel that these women dumb themselves down in order to gain social acceptance. These girls that are so smart—student body presidents, lettering in sports, top of their class—are letting the men set the social standards. The men determine the role of the women by setting the rules and expectations that the women try to live up to—and the women let them.

One of the girls interviewed confessed that she had done things that went completely against who she was and what she valued. There was one guy that she hooked up with that wouldn't let her go anywhere social without him, but would go to parties and do stuff without her all the time. She stayed with him for a whole year, because she felt lucky to be with him and was afraid of losing him.

Many of the girls had done similar things and felt ashamed of the way they had behaved, but justified it the same way: They felt that they were lucky to have scored a hook-up with a cool frat guy, and they needed to do whatever they had to in order to get it and maintain it. The girls also claimed that it never went the other way. The guy was never lucky to be with the girl, and never had to be afraid of losing the girl, no matter how gorgeous or intelligent she was.

One girl said that it was especially upsetting due to the fact that the women at the college tended to look down on the frat guys as slackers, and that most of them weren't even good looking. She said that there were only

three or four of them that she would say were 'hot.' Yet, if she saw one of those short, "scrunchy" guys with a gorgeous model-looking girl, she would think, "Oh, she's so lucky to have him."[3]

She went on to explain that she found herself in a situation with a guy that made her "very uncomfortable and unhappy, because it's not a way to live. But if I didn't do these things and he broke up with me for some reason, two days from now he'd have somebody else."[4]

These extraordinary women admit that they are downplaying themselves so that they can be in "uncomfortable and unhappy" relationships with guys that they "look down on." It seems so ludicrous as to be impossible to believe. And it gets worse.

The girls say that all of the sexual activity at the school happens in what they call a "hook-up", which could be anything from making-out to actual sex. Students at the university—guys and girls—say that there really isn't much of a real dating scene. Usually there is just drinking and one night stands. One girl (described in the article as a "stunning brunette"[5]) admitted that she had never been asked out, and that guys hadn't even ever bought her a drink.

There is no pretext of the guy trying to impress the girl by asking her out, dressing up nice, or buying her dinner. There are just casual hook-ups—one night stands followed by nothing. One girl said that the best you could hope for was to hook-up with that guy again, and maybe even turn it into a regular hook-up (which just means consistent sex for the guy, not really a relationship), but most girls just bounce around between guys.

These women work hard to be awesome and beautiful, and what do they get for it? Respect? Love? Free Dinner? NOTHING!!! They get a "hook-up." The guys they are hooking up with aren't even that attractive. The best thing these women can hope to gain from all of their effort is a one-night stand with a guy that only cares about what kind of sex the girl is going to offer.

This is a stark illustration of where the feminist movement failed. In trying to make women equal with men, they tried to make women the same as men. Men had "sexual freedom," and they felt women needed that also. In gaining this so-called "sexual freedom," they also achieved what men have enjoyed for thousands of years—emotional starvation. You cannot separate sex and relationships, or at least not in any sort of healthy manner. It's like separating food and nutrition. The primary purpose of eating is for nourishment. There is some food that tastes good, to be sure. There is also food that isn't as good, though it is necessary to good health. If a person confuses the purpose of eating to be only for self-pleasure and taste, and completely disregards the nutritional needs of their body, they are going to get sick.

A person that has sex for fun, with no regard for the emotional consequences of such an intimate act, will soon find themselves in a similarly unhealthy situation emotionally. Men have subjected themselves to this for thousands of years. Prior to the feminist movement, it was acceptable for men to have sex in a variety of ways with a variety of women. Men could go to strip clubs, hire whores, and keep mistresses. I'm not saying it was advertised, but it was tolerated. "Men will be men, after all," or at least that is how society rationalized such behavior. Women, on the other hand, could only have sex with their husbands. Society would approve of nothing else, and feminists saw this as unfair. They wanted the same "sexual freedom" as men.

However, by giving in to his every desire, many a man has become a sex 'junkie,' willing to disregard everything in order to get his next fix. In winning sexual freedom, many women have managed to debase themselves in the same way. They can have just as much sex as men, which will result in just as few meaningful and fulfilling relationships. Sexual freedom gives men and women one thing—sex. But sex alone, without discipline and void of emotion, is unhealthy. It does not give lasting joy. It does not nourish happiness or lead to human fulfillment.

There is yet another complication to this problem. Feminism, in trying to level the playing field between men and women, introduced women to a game that will never be fair as long as it is played by the same rules that men follow. Men and women are physically different, and therefore physically unequal. That might sound politically incorrect to say, but you'll find the proof in any anatomy textbook. The reason the Olympics are still separated by gender is because men and women are not physically equal. Given the same sport and the same rules, one gender will have an advantage over the other. This applies to anything physical. Math and writing and science may be the same for either sex, but sports, health, and childbirth are not. You can't take something physical and apply the same rules to both men and women and expect equality to be the result. The only way men and women can have no advantage over each other is if each side has a different set of rules that accommodates the strengths and weakness of that particular gender.

Sex is no different. Men and women cannot operate under the same rules and conditions and have equality. Men have been endeavoring to shape the rules to their advantage for thousands of years. For the most part, they have succeeded. However, recent centuries saw a shift in standards that gave women more power and freedom than they had before, and established a delicate balance as women struggled for new freedoms and men longed for the old repressions. Then, in its quest to make men value women as equals, feminism entered women into a game designed for women to lose. In winning sexual emancipation, women lost the respect and power they had been struggling for so long to gain.

This is clearly portrayed in the article's description of

a very popular frat party, called WWIII. At this party freshmen are initiated into the fraternity by women who are invited to do the hazing. Two of the women interviewed had been invited to one such party, and were excited to go because the guys had chosen *them*. It was an honor because only the hottest girls were invited.

WWIII is a progressive party that advances from one room to another. Each room has a different theme and a new set of girls. In one room, where the theme was Dazed and Confused, the girls wore low cut t-shirts (very tight, of course), short shorts, and whistles. When the freshmen guys came in (wearing just their boxers), the girls would haze them by shouting at them and giving them orders. Some girls would straddle the boys dominatrix style and call them babies or yell obscenities at them. Other girls would smear their chests with chocolate syrup and whipped cream and then make the guys lick it off.

Some women see this as a role reversal where the girls get to boss the guys around for a change, but one guy— a member of a different fraternity—admitted that the whole thing was very demeaning. Another professor agreed, pointing out that the girls are just fulfilling the guys' fantasies, and putting themselves in a subservient role. Many of the girls don't see it that way, though. They think it is a powerful experience over the guys. One girl even said, "It's kind of like domination through sex."[6]

Do you remember the title of Chapter Two? Here are very intelligent women who are completely clueless when it comes to men and sex. They are so completely naïve that they honestly believe that they have "power" at that party. I'm sure every man's insecurity stems from a fear that a gorgeous woman will force him to lick whipped cream off of her bare chest. Wake up, Ladies!

Have you ever read Tom Sawyer? Remember the part where Tom, assigned the dreadful task of whitewashing a fence, convinces all of the other boys that they should pay him for the opportunity to help whitewash the fence? I'm sure Mark Twain would be shocked to see how far this fraternity has taken that ploy. These boys invite hot women to a party where the women 'force' the boys to participate in sexual activities. And the women feel honored to have been invited. So honored, in fact, that they will do everything the guys ask. How powerful does that sound?

It can all be summed up by a statement made by one of the girls as she watched students at a popular campus hangout. She says that when she looks at the girls she thinks 'wow,' but when she looks at the guys there she just has to say no.

She says, "I feel like in the real world, these guys would never be with these girls—they're way too beautiful. And way too intelligent."[7]

Way too beautiful? Probably. Way too intelligent?

Apparently not, because the same thing happens in the "real world" all the time. Gorgeous and talented women give themselves up to swaggering men at all ages, selling themselves short because some Jerk is over-inflated.

Chapter Eight

How to Snag a Nice Guy

Finally, the chapter you've all been waiting for. I am going to tell you exactly how to find a Nice Guy, and how to get a date with him. Got your pencils ready? His name is Alan. He's a really good friend of mine, and a great guy. He's also an excellent cook. He's pretty much free every night, so give him a call. His number is…

Just kidding. If only finding the Man-of-Your-Dreams was that easy, right? Unfortunately, there is no book that lists nice single guys, along with their hobbies and phone numbers, though that would make a good sequel. For now, all I can give you are a few strategies for finding that special Nice Guy.

It doesn't matter what age or what gender a person is, there are two basic problems when it comes to relationships with the opposite sex. The first problem is not being able to meet anybody. The second is meeting too many of the wrong somebody's. If you don't fall into either of these categories, chances are you're an amoeba.

Unlike amoebas, whose entire dating life—from cell make-up to cell break-up—has been carefully documented by researchers, there is no exact science for human relationships. The strategies I am about to give are not a guaranteed recipe for lasting happiness. They are simply good advice, and it is up to you to tailor them to fit your own personality and situation.

Strategy #1: Define 'Fine'

Regardless of the approach you take to men, the first thing you need to decide is what you want. As cheesy as this may sound, you need to make a list. Not only that, you need to write your list down. Here's why.

Most women truly want men that will make them happy. They want men who will respect them and treat them with kindness. They want men who will love them, and care for them. Women have their dream men, but settle for 'real men' only to wake up in a nightmare. The reality is that the man standing in front of you, giving flashy smiles and flattering comments, will always seem better than a Mr. Perfect who has not even entered the scene yet. Even if Mr. Perfect is on stage, a really smooth Player can usually find a way to steal the show before the curtain comes down. Suave and sweet-talking, Players know how to make women forget what they really want, and settle for what looks good at the moment. They're like chocolate when you're on a diet—smooth and sweet right now, but they're not going to help you feel better about yourself in the end.

Just like when you are on a diet, you need goals to remind you of what you really want. If you don't want the wrong guy turning your romantic comedy into a tragedy, you need to script out your happy ending right now. Write down exactly what will make you happy. Lay out the qualities that you value most in a guy. Set standards for yourself—what a man must have to be worthy of you, what he must do to win your love, and what he is absolutely forbidden to do if he wants your affection.

I asked a couple of girl friends if it would be okay if I shared some items off of their lists with you. To protect their identities and their lists, I have combined the items into one list, which I will pretend belongs to a girl named Mary. The original lists were divided into different sections, depending on how important something was, so I have divided this list up similarly.

The first category is traits that the guy must have in order to get any consideration at all. Mary will not even entertain the idea of having a relationship with a guy that fails to possess all of these traits. It may sound a little harsh, but this is one of the two most important categories. You need to seriously consider what is essential to your future happiness. Do you want kids? Do you absolutely have to live in California? What about religion and politics—are those negotiable? Because this category is non-negotiable, you need to be careful what you include in it. Don't put anything that you are not willing to stand firm on.

The second category is things that are very important, but might have a little room for forgiveness. A man with everything from this section would be awesome, and a man with only a few things is due to get dumped. Since Mary understands that no one is perfect, she's willing to let a guy slide on a few things, but the guy needs to have most of these qualities.

Next are the things that would be grand. This is where Mary goes crazy, thinking of all the things that would

make a guy perfectly dreamy. These items are not necessary in any way, but Mary wanted to put them down because she was having fun imagining what her perfect guy would be like.

Finally, there are the deal-breakers. This is the other all-important category. These are the things Mary will not accept. No matter how dreamy the guy is, or how well he measures up in all other categories, if his character suffers from one of these afflictions, he's history. Once again, there is no room for compromise in this category, so be very careful what you include in it.

Now that you understand what the categories are, here is Mary's list:

Mary's List

Absolutely Positively Unequivocally Must:
Want children.
Be a strong, active Christian.
Have a good sense of humor, without treating everything like a joke.
Make her feel like a woman in the way he treats her and adores her.
Be sensitive enough to have a deep conversation about feelings every once in a while.
Have a career goal and a strong sense of direction for where he wants to go in life.

Needs at least Eight out of Ten:
Be older/more mature than she is.
Be one step ahead of her—a little bit smarter, a little bit fitter, a little bit more spiritual, etc.
Be able to take sarcasm.
Be a virgin.
Like to play sports and be physically active.
Enjoy theater.
Like similar music.
Have a good relationship with his family.
Play an instrument.
Have similar political views.

Wouldn't Life be Grand if He:
Had any color of eyes besides brown.
Felt comfortable in a suit and liked to dress up.
Had a good voice and enjoyed singing.
Had muscular arms.
Had a foreign accent.
Spoke another language.

Any of the Following Will Result in Automatic and Immediate Disqualification, Without Appeal or Exception:
Cheating.
Dishonesty.

Picking up hookers, hiring strippers, or going to
a nudie bar.
Verbal or physical abuse.
Smoking.
Getting Drunk.
Using Drugs.

I'm not giving this as an example of what a perfect list
would look like (that would be my wife's list)—I just want
you to see what kinds of things might be on a list to give
you some ideas. Every woman is going to have different
needs and different desires. Make your list to match what
will make *you* truly happy.

It is also very important to realize that your list is
probably going to change. As people grow up, things
change. Lessons learned from past relationships may
change what you want in future ones. It is okay to change
your list in such a case, but only *between* relationships!

While you are in a relationship, treat that list like it is
written in stone. When some dreamy-lookin', smooth-
talkin' Jerk tries to sail you through a fog of flattery, your
list is the anchor that will keep you out of deep water. If
you start changing your list to match the man of the
moment, you are letting him pirate your hopes and happiness, and your ship is sunk. Instead, politely pass on any
guy that doesn't measure up to your specifications, and

when you are no longer under his influence in any way, if you still feel the list needs a change, then go for it. However, I can almost promise you that you will rarely feel the need to change the list once you are over what's-his-name.

Strategy #2: Be a Nice Girl

This includes a lot of things, many of which I have already mentioned, but are worth going over again briefly. First of all, looks are important. You need to look nice. By 'nice' I mean somewhere between sloppy and slutty. Don't overdo it with short skirts, revealing shirts, and too much makeup. But don't belittle yourself with messy hair and sloppy clothes. Wear clothes that show you care about yourself, but won't draw guys' eyes away from your smile.

Speaking of smiles, try to always keep one on you. To a Nice Guy, your face is far more important than your figure. If you have a confident and happy look, Nice Guys will notice. If you don't have a super sexy figure, *and* you look like you hate life, then it just looks like you hate yourself for being ugly. If you have a smile and you look like you love life, then you don't need to worry about being ugly, because no Nice Guy will ever think you are. A smile is the cheapest miracle-makeover you can give yourself.

Now that you are smiling, it should be easy to be nice to the people around you. You don't have to spend your life working in orphanages, just be polite and kind to the people around you—*all* of the people around you. Be nice to pretty people and ugly people, the jocks and the dorks, the famous and the homeless. Say please and thank you, hold the door for people, and give out compliments. Soon you will find yourself in a nicer world, with much nicer guys.

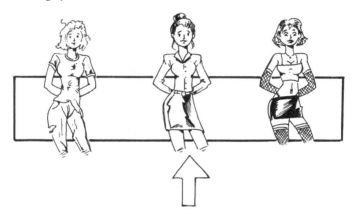

Strategy #3: Establish a "No Fly Zone"

Have you ever been to a picnic or barbeque and dished up a really tasty looking dessert, but before you ate it you had to go get another glass of lemonade, and by the time you got back, your dessert was completely covered in flies? Did it make your dessert look a little less appetizing?

Like the dessert, you are sweet and attractive—and you will probably attract far more bad than good. Guys

around you will try to get your attention by "hovering" over you like flies. Also like that dessert, if you let any guy passing by hover near you trying to get your attention, you will end up being unattractive to the Nice Guys you are hoping to meet. Remember, Nice Guys are easily intimidated. If a Nice Guy is interested in a girl, but she is constantly surrounded by Jerks, he'll assume two things. First, that his chances of successfully competing for her attention are essentially zero. Second, that anything surrounded by flies might already be tainted. With a small sigh of remorse, he'll give up.

You need to keep the "flies" away from you. Swat them, shoo them, do whatever you have to do to get rid of them. I'm not saying that you should be mean. Treating men like dirt and acting like you are too good for them will only give you the reputation of being a snob. That will not help your situation. Instead, be nice. Smile. But turn them down, stop their advances, and stay out of relationships.

This will have two major advantages. The first is that you will appear completely free to any Nice Guy who is trying to work up the courage to talk to you. Second, nothing boosts the confidence of a Nice Guy like seeing a Jerk get rejected. If you shoot down every Jerk that makes a play for you, you will be the hero of Nice Guys everywhere. I'm serious. You'll become a legend. Every Nice Guy that hears about you will say, "Finally, a woman who *gets it*. A woman who understands what men are after. A woman who respects herself. Why can't all women be like *her*?!!"

And maybe in the next year or so, one of those Nice Guys will work up enough courage to talk to you. If you don't want to wait that long, then you'll need an additional strategy.

Strategy #4: Don't Just Stand There!

Nice Guys are notoriously shy. You can complain that it makes life difficult and wait for it to change, and you can die old and lonely, too. Or you can just deal with the fact that they are shy, and make the first move.

Just don't make it a hasty move. If you move too fast you run the risk of two mistakes. First, you might be chasing a Jerk that you thought was a Nice Guy. Take the time to make sure of your target. Second, Nice Guys are used to being attacked and ridiculed, and if you just come out of nowhere and start trying to notice him, he might think that you are trying to set him up for a joke.

So make your move, but do it their way. First, take your time and pay attention so that you know who the Nice Guys really are. Then slowly work your way into their comfort zone. If they sit across the cafeteria from you, sit at the table next to them for a week. Then start saying hi to them before you sit down at your table. Then get up and talk to them as you coincidentally go to throw something away at the same time as them. Spend a week or so of just saying hi and exchanging small talk whenever you pass them, and then try sitting at their table. Then just be their friend.

This approach, while slow and sometimes frustrating, has a couple of advantages. First, it gives you plenty of time to measure the guy up as you slowly get to know him. If you change your mind, you can slowly fade out without hurting anyone's feelings. Second, since you aren't committing to a relationship, you can work on getting to be friends with three or four Nice Guys at a time. It takes the same amount of time as getting to know one, but having three Nice Guys as friends just gives you a lot more options. Be friends with them all for a while, hanging out and having fun. Those Nice Guys will introduce you to more Nice Guys (they tend to hang out with each other) and pretty soon you'll find that you are friends with a lot of really nice guys.

Now that you are friends with a lot of Nice Guys, you have three choices. One, you can just enjoy being their friends until you are really ready to move into a relationship. Two, you can make the classic female blunder and ignore all of them and their warnings and decide to date some Jerk. Three, you can date and fall in love with one of them. If you take option number one, you can use that time to gradually coach them out of dorkiness. But even if you choose number one, eventually you'll have to choose between number two and three. If you choose option two, just know that those Nice Guys will be there for you when you get dumped or divorced, but they will probably be in their own relationships by then, and you will have missed your chance. So to make everyone's life easier, just go with option three, and live happily ever after. I don't have much more advice on how to do that, but there is a nice story about it in the last chapter.

Strategy #5: No Kissing!

So you found the Nice Guy of your dreams and you have started dating. There is a good chance that you are his first girl friend, and that he will be experiencing a lot of new emotions and feelings. Don't screw him up, and your relationship, by moving too fast with things. Even a Nice Guy has hormones, and if you get into kissing, there is the possibility that he could succumb to those hormones and end up doing something that a Jerk would do. Unlike a Jerk, he would regret it terribly, but it would pretty much be the end of you and him together.

Obviously, if you are going to live happily ever after, then there will be kissing. Just make sure that your relationship is solid before you go that direction. If your relationship can't withstand not kissing, then it will definitely be a disaster after you start kissing. So use some self-control and take things slowly. If you are really meant for each other, you will have the rest of your lives together to exchange smooches.

Finally, set ground rules of what you are each comfortable with and what you want before each transition into a deeper relationship. Working together to make your relationship rewarding for both of you will set a precedent of making each other happy for the rest of your lives.

Chapter Nine

The Definition of a Woman

This book started out being all about guys. Perhaps it seems strange that it has turned into a book about women. The truth is that it has always been about you, ladies. *You* are what makes the world go 'round. And the world largely revolves around you. Men work and sweat and save and sacrifice and bleed and die for women. They may not respect you the way they should. Many may prefer to keep you as sluts and slaves instead of equals. But it doesn't change the fact that men need women. Men desperately long for women. Men seek money and power and nice cars so that they can have women. Many a man has lost everything over a woman.

Being so important, it should come as no surprise to you that there are a lot of different people trying to define what you should be and how you should act. Everyone wants to define your place in the world, and there are a hundred different roles that the various powers that be would have you play.

The extreme conservatives define women as subservient housewives. A woman should stay home and tend the chores and children, and provide all of the comforts of the softer sex to her husband. She should spend her youth learning to cook and clean and clip out coupons. Her love should be her children, and her loyalty should be to her husband.

The extreme liberals would define a woman as ambitious, driven by all of the things that drive men. A woman should want success and power. She is defined by her career and shouldn't allow a husband or children to distract her from that. She shuns everything traditional about womanhood. She is supposed to be everything a man is thought to be, and she is supposed to do it in a superior way.

And then you have everything in between. Movies define women as being perfectly shaped and impeccably fashionable. T.V. shows define older women as nags, middle age women as smarter than their husbands, and younger women as easy. There are people to tell you that you are too fat, and people to tell you you're too thin. You might have heard that women are smarter than men, or maybe someone told you that women aren't very good at math.

Some people say women are the gentler sex—kind

and caring, naturally inclined to nurture. Others say that women just want sex, and that they only pretended to care about relationships because society forced it upon them. Pornography defines you as a sex toy. Abusive and bullying men define you as weak, and make sure you know it.

Everywhere a young woman turns there is another person with another opinion about how she should act, what she should wear, who she should love, why she should care, or where she should be going. And for all of this advice, women haven't seemed to make themselves a whole lot happier.

The tricky thing about discovering and defining who you are is that you have to explore different options and seek new experiences—which always increases the risk of doing something really stupid. Some people have wise parents or a strong religious conviction to help them avoid the most common mistakes. Other people have no such role model, and their lives are scarred by the consequences of tragic errors.

I'm not going to pretend to be the hero that can save all of womankind. I have no superpowers, and when I take off my glasses it doesn't make me unrecognizable. Rather, without my glasses, everyone else becomes unrecognizable. And I trip over stuff. Still, I want to offer some advice, in the hope that it can help in some small way.

There have been thousands of pages written on the subject of "finding oneself," so there isn't a whole lot that

I can say that is new. However, I do have one piece of wisdom that I thought of on my own, and I have never read anywhere else. It is a basic rule of thumb that I apply whenever I am making decisions. It goes like this:

If something is easy to get into and hard to get out of, then it is probably bad.

If something is hard to get into and easy to get out of, then it is probably okay.

This bit of wisdom is based on my belief that the most important thing a person can have is freedom. You cannot be happy without freedom. In order to define yourself you must be free to choose your actions. Following this logic, any

Easy to get into...

Hard to get out.

choice that potentially limits your freedom in the future is one that should be considered very carefully. Conversely, the choices that expand your opportunities are probably a good way to go. Consider these examples:

Robbing a Bank—it is relatively easy to walk into a bank with a gun. It is much harder to get back out, and a lifetime in prison for armed robbery severely limits your future options.

Going to College—maintaining a good GPA, saving up money, and filling out applications are all grueling tasks. Giving up and dropping out is a piece of cake. But a college graduate reaps the benefits of advanced opportunities for the rest of their life.

Smoking—it's almost as easy as breathing to start. Some people spend their whole lives trying to quit. A person who hasn't ever smoked still has the choice whether or not to have a cigarette. Smokers only get to choose their brand.

Starting a Savings Account—as your money grows, the number of things you can buy with it grows even faster.

A One Night Stand—five minutes of reckless abandon can lead to a number of lifelong consequences, almost all of which require a doctor and cost money.

Learning a New Language—A person that can speak English, Spanish, and Mandarin Chinese can have a conversation with over 80% of the people in the world. (If you only speak French, there probably isn't anybody that wants to talk to you.)

It isn't a perfect rule. For instance, joining the army is fairly easy, while getting out can be almost impossible, and you lose a lot of privileges while you are a soldier. I joined the Army anyway, but only after a lot of research and careful consideration, and I'm glad I did it. The point of the rule is not to blindly label everything good or bad. The point is for you think about consequences, and about how a choice will affect your freedom. If you do that with every decision you have to make, you'll safely navigate your way through the more difficult choices in life, and reap the benefits of being truly free to pursue happiness throughout your life.

A second piece of advice that I would like to offer to women seeking to define themselves is this:

As a woman, you are different than a man.

I know it seems obvious, but a lot of women forget this. Don't waste your life and talents trying to impress and outdo men. Let men have their own chest beating contests. You are a woman. Men should not define you and your relationships. If you allow that, you will be constantly unhappy. If you try to play the game their way, you will most likely lose. Like I pointed out in chapter seven, when you are physically different, you can't play a physical game by the same rules and be equal. Eagles fly, and dolphins swim. If either one tries to outdo the other, they will fall short.

It is very difficult to force the people around you to change. Strangely enough (and I've never been able to quite figure out how this paradox works) it is much easier to let others change you. Sometimes those influences are good; sometimes they are bad. If you are an eagle, its okay to let the dolphin convince you to try fish, but don't let him make you think you should give up flying so that you can live with him in the ocean. The key to happiness in a relationship is to make compromises without compromising yourself.

Currently, most of the men out there are selfish, immature Jerks. As a solitary person, there is little you can do to change that. But don't let it change you. Decide who you are. Become who you want to be. Do it for yourself, not for anyone else. Then keep all of your relationships in the context of who you are. Don't play the Player's game. If a man wants to have anything to do with you, make him play your game. You'll know you've found a good match when you find a man whose rules mesh with your rules to form a game that is fair for both of you, and allow each of you to be who you really are.

Letting other people tell you what to be is not the only danger in the quest for self-discovery. Sometimes people find a special talent or interest early on in their life and immediately attach themselves to it. Discovering that you are smart, athletic, or artistic can lead to a temptation to define yourself by that attribute. It's there, you're reasonably good at it, so why not? It makes life easy to find something so defining early on. However, you are a whole person, not a lone talent. Trying to define your entire self with a single skill or attribute is like balancing precariously on one leg. So find your second leg—branch out. Do some research and try different things. Don't be afraid of finding out what you are not good at. Most people are bad at more things than they are good at. Accept that, and be enthusiastic in your search for new talents.

During your search, you're probably going to start feeling like life is too short. Only people going nowhere ever feel like they have time to get there. Those of us trying to be better start to feel that by the time we have made all of our mistakes and learned all of our lessons, we'll already be dead. Is there a way to live life faster and find ourselves quicker so that we still have some time left over at the end?

According to the Population Reference Bureau, approximately 60 billion people have lived on earth in the last 2,000 years. That is a lot of life experience that has preceded us, and a lot of it has been written down. Reading about someone else's life can be a quick way of learning a life's worth of lessons. During my late teens and early twenties, I read a lot of biographies. I read about people I admired, and I read about people I despised. Many of their experiences resonated with my own. I found things that I wanted to make part of me. I found characteristics that I wanted nothing to do with. I found inspiration to make it through difficult experiences.

Besides reading biographies, I tried to observe the people around me. I watched people that I respected to see what I could learn from them. I even found that I could learn a lot from people I didn't like. One of the greatest examples of teaching I have ever seen came from a man that I am sure was certifiably crazy.

The point is that we are not alone. As we try to define ourselves, we don't have to write an entire dictionary from scratch. Nor should we just copy someone else's. Just take those things that inspire and excite you—things that already feel like they are part of you, and let those things become part of how you define yourself.

Finally, *finding* self-definition is not the only difficult thing. Sticking with what you believe you are can be just as hard. It means that your primary source of self-esteem must be yourself. This is one of the keys to lasting happiness. A lot of people place their entire sense of self worth into one area of their life, and it rarely turns out well. Many nerds measure their value in how many people they are smarter than. If they meet someone smarter than them, it knocks their own value down a notch. There are girls who take all of their self-esteem from how pretty they are. If they meet someone prettier than them, it makes them insecure, bitter, and competitive. I knew men in the army that were defined by their rank. Having a high rank made them feel superior and important. When they left the army they became depressed, because no one in the civilian world cared about their previous rank.

If you cling to one constricted definition, if you base your self-esteem on the first thing you think you are good at, you will find your life on a narrow foundation that is easily toppled over. Read, watch, listen—find ways to branch out, and define yourself with values that are part of you and can't be taken away.

Don't base all of your self worth on something that someone can take away from you—especially if you are in a relationship with that someone. Girls that define themselves by how popular, handsome, or cool their boyfriend is give away all of their power and freedom. If he leaves, they become nothing. They see themselves as worthless without that man. So they will do everything to keep him. However, since he doesn't need her, he can do anything he wants, because she needs him, and he knows it. She will tolerate lies, neglect, and abuse, because anything is better than being worth nothing.

Before you seek happiness with a guy, find it within yourself first. If you cannot be happy alone, it means that you are missing something that someone else can't give you. Find yourself. Define who you are as your own entity. When you know who you are you will be able to find the right guy. You will make each other happy, just the way you are.

Chapter Ten

Starting a Revolution

During the writing of this book, I have shared a lot of my ideas with my friends to see what they think. Most of the girls that I have shared this with have had the same response: What you say is true, but it's not going to change the way that girls act, so your book is pointless.

I have had to sadly acknowledge that they are probably right. While I didn't let it stop me from writing the book, it still continues to bother me. I would like to take a moment now to try and address this concern.

The way I see it, the reason that girls probably aren't going to change when they read this book is because if they follow the advice I give, they will most likely end up as social outcasts. I know saying that isn't going to help my case very much, but we all know it is true. I also know, from personal experience, that it is not a whole lot of fun being an outcast. For all of you women trying to figure out how to balance your social status with a happy relationship, I have two things to say.

First, right now there are a whole lot of Nice Guys out there who are experiencing some degree of social exile because they are Nice Guys. There are certain things that they won't do because they are Nice Guys, and other things they always do because they are Nice Guys, and many of the things in each of those categories make them un-cool and unpopular. Everyday when they wake up they could choose to give up their values and join the in-crowd, but instead they choose to stand up for what they believe is important, knowing what the social consequences will be. If you decide that changing your life is too hard or too dangerous to your social status, then that is your choice. Just remember that when you settle for lower standards for yourself, you are settling for lower standards in the people around you. So before you start complaining about how there are no Nice Guys in the world, remember that it was you who was too afraid to go find them.

Second, it's about time that you women quit letting men run the world. Nice Guys can't change the whole world because there just aren't enough of them. Men in general aren't going to change things because by their below-the-belt way of thinking, the current state of affairs works really well for them. The only ones who have the incentive and the numbers to change the world are women. The only way that women are going to change things is if they motivate themselves and come together.

Not very long ago I had a conversation with three girls—juniors in high school—who were very upset. In one of their classes they had been talking to some boys—all of whom had girlfriends—and these guys had agreed that if a certain girl (we'll call her Valerie) ever came up to them and offered a one night stand, they would take it—even if they were married and had kids, they said.

Well, that made these girls pretty upset, and an argument ensued. During the argument the guys admitted that they had no long-term plans for any of their girl-friends. In fact, their plan was to leave town and go to college and have as much fun as they could with as many different girls as possible while in college. They saw no reason to limit themselves to just one girl.

The girls argued that eventually the guys would want to settle down, and that getting around in college was only going to burn their bridges and leave them with no opportunity for a real relationship because all of the girls would know that they were Jerks. The guys' rebuttal was that even if that happened, they could just come back to their hometown because the girls here would always be here and would always take them back. At that point the bell rang, ending the exchange.

With their anger unappeased, the girls now wanted my opinion on the whole issue.

"Well," I said, "I'm happy to hear that they are planning

on going to college." Up to that point I wasn't sure that any of those guys had any plans for the future, so it was good to hear that college was in their sights.

"That's not the question!" objected the girls.

"Right. Well, I agree with you. They're Jerks. But the problem is that they're right, and they know it, and you know it, which is why you're so mad."

I braced myself for impact, but surprisingly, they assented. Still upset, they asked me what could be done about it. Was there a way to make the world fair and knock the smug heads right off of those conceited little punks? We didn't have time to resolve that question right then, but I assured them it could be done. The problem is, it can't be done alone.

If one girl reads this book and decides to change the way she acts and the guys she dates, she's going to experience a lot of rejection as all the Jerks shun her, and other girls make fun of her. But one day she will meet a Nice Guy and it will have all been worth it for both of them because they will be happy while the rest of the world will continue to be miserable.

If all of the girls in a community read this book and decided to change together, then the guys in that community would have a problem. The players would find that their game was over. When they decided that one girl was too goody-goody for them, they wouldn't be able to bounce to the next one, because none of them would be falling for it. They would try to fake being a Nice Guy, but if the girls stuck to the rules then that ploy wouldn't work. Eventually, the guys would either have to change or leave town. The ones who stuck around would have to show a whole lot more respect to the girls around them, and the girls would find that they were in a lot better situation than they were before. If each generation of girls in that community stuck to their commitment, eventually the men in the community would change, because the younger boys would never learn the predatory habits of the generations before them.

That can only work if girls stop fighting with each other and turn their fury on the men that take advantage of them and their stupidity. I'm sick and tired of hearing girls blame each other for men cheating on them. If your boyfriend cheats on you, it's not the other girl's fault for being a slut (even if she is); it's *HIS* fault for being an unfaithful, cheating sack of slime. Turn your rage on him, and every man like him. Stop fighting with each other, women. You are not in a competition with each other. As long as you try to beat each other, the only prize you are going to win is that aforementioned sack of worthless slime. If you're so anxious to have it, just go scrape some off the walls of the gym's shower. At least that stuff will never treat you wrong.

The true enemy—the opponent that you must over-come—is all of the Jerks out there who think you are stupid, know you have low self-esteem, and feel that they can treat you any way they want because there will always be another girl just as dumb down the road.

The guys from the conversation before knew that they were totally safe. They knew that there would always be girls dumb enough or desperate enough to take them, no matter how much they advertised their complete disrespect for women. But imagine if that was the day that girls at that school decided they had had enough. What if that was the day all the girls decided that they were tired of being the ones that got dumped and cheated on, tired of being the ones called sluts and whores, tired of being the ones who had to drop out of school to raise a kid because they "proved their love" to guys that never loved or respected them. What if it was that day? Can you imagine it?

That would be the day that those guys never got another date with another girl in that town. They wouldn't ever consider renting a hotel room on prom night again because they wouldn't ever have a date to prom. It wouldn't matter if they were football stars, because cheering would be the extent of the cheerleaders' extracurricular activities. Those guys' social life would be over. The popular girls wouldn't date them. The unpopular girls wouldn't date them. That would be the day they lost that smug, perverted grin off of their conceited little faces. It would also be the day that all of the guys in that school decided they better be a whole heck of a lot nicer—before X-box became their only option on a Friday night.

Now imagine if women and girls all over the country decided to take a stand together. What if the united front of feminism was one of self-respect and complete rejection of all things disrespectful to women? If women came together to do that—if they all decided at once that they were going to respect themselves and demand the same from men—it would change the world.

Men have always had somewhere else to run for fun. They have always counted on the fact that there would always be a stupid woman somewhere that they could take advantage of. There have always been easy women for men to have their way with, which meant that if any woman took a stand, she would find herself isolated as men turned to easier ways of getting their pleasure. If, however, men suddenly found all of those doors closed to them, their world would come crumbling down.

If girls didn't stand for backstabbing and insults from each other, then they would quit allowing it from men, as well. Women, instead of conditioning yourselves to be lied to and trampled on by always doing it to each other, try respecting each other, liking each other, sticking up for each other. When you come to expect that from each other, then you will quit accepting anything less from men. Girls spend so much time insecure about themselves because of the way other girls treat them that when a guy comes in and does something remotely nice, she goes head over heels for him. Women have set themselves up to be easily taken advantage of, and men have proven that they are more than willing to oblige.

If, instead of ripping each other apart, women supported and encouraged one another to believe in themselves and respect themselves, there wouldn't be an entire class of disenfranchised women willing to work for pimps on street corners, in strip clubs, or on porn sites. If women took a stand of self-respect together, then men would find all of their easy outlets cut off, and they would have to start to change.

Some wouldn't, of course, but they would become the social outcasts, while being a nice guy and a nice girl would become the norm. Boys would grow up knowing that they had to respect women, and they would learn that anything less than that would get them nothing. Girls would grow up believing that they were worth something, and getting the respect they deserved.

I know that it sounds like a fairy tale—too good to be true. It is not up to me to decide how it all will end. Each of you girls reading this has to decide whether or not things will change. You can ignore me. You can try to fight it alone. Or you can try to spread it until it turns into a revolution, forever shifting the balance of power.

In the end, while I dream of a world where a Nice Guy

can carry a briefcase and still get a date, I know that I may never live to see that day. However, if my advice can help just one girl avoid a devastating relationship or a heartbreaking mistake, then this book will not have killed a tree in vain. And for that I will be glad.

"Happily Ever After"

I've talked a lot about the sacrifices that Nice Guys (and nice girls) have to make in order to find true love and happiness, but I'm afraid I've made too big a deal of the down side of that, and not focused enough on the rewards. You probably can't imagine that I'm the one to tell you about "happily ever after." I'm the dork that carried a briefcase to school, got picked on, and couldn't get a date in high school, right?

Right. But let me tell you the rest of the story. As I've mentioned before, the reason that Nice Guys appear aloof sometimes (or in my case, most of the time) is because they have a different outlook on life and different goals. That was me. I was always looking to the long term. I saw junior high and high school as a temporary phase and an obnoxious impediment to getting on with my real life. I had hopes and dreams and goals that I wanted to fulfill, and none of them involved anything that was happening in high school, other than the fact that I needed good grades in order to pay for college. Meanwhile, the furthest ahead any of my classmates were thinking was with whom they would go to prom.

As a result, I looked like a dork. Now I have to admit that I wasn't trying to look like a dork. I won't claim to be one of those people that didn't care what other people thought of me. I always wished that I wasn't the one getting snickered at or made the butt of jokes. I tried not to be a complete geek in the way I acted and dressed. But the truth was that with the goal I was headed toward, I just couldn't devote enough time and resources to keeping up with how to be cool. So I accepted that during the temporary tortures known as junior high and high school I would not be a popular person.

This is not to say I was a complete loner. I had friends—good friends. Really nice people that stuck together and helped each other and never turned on each other like so many friends do in high school. And, with the exception of a few jocks and bullies, I got along with people. As the Nice Guy, there were a lot of girls that would confide in me and ask me for advice or help on homework—they just wouldn't ever consider going out with me.

Not that I got the guts up very often to ask. Besides, I had some goals in life that didn't involve girls, so while I would have enjoyed a little more attention from them, I knew that it was better that I stayed uninvolved for the time being. It was just one of the sacrifices I decided I needed to make for something that was more important.

Two things that were more important, actually. First, I wanted to be a full time minister and missionary for my church. I knew that for that period of time I would have to be focused and work hard, and leave any relationships behind until I was finished. Besides, I was going to be a volunteer clergyman, so I needed to save up as much money as possible to live off of during my time of service. Nice cars and fancy dates didn't fit into that picture. I spent two years in China after I graduated, and every moment of that was worth everything I sacrificed in high school to get there. I met many people who touched my life, and I was able to help a few of them in return.

After returning from China, I immediately enlisted in the Army Reserves. That may not sound like a huge commitment, but I signed up to be a Respiratory Therapist, which required over a year of active duty training. The first two and a half months of training were spent at Ft. Benning, Georgia—Home of the Infantry. Fort Benning is an all-male basic training site, and my platoon is where all of the future respiratory therapists were assigned, so I got to know all of the other guys pretty well. From Georgia all of us respiratory guys shipped off to Texas together to attend our medical training. That is where we associated with women for the first time in over two months.

The first company we were assigned to consisted of two hundred soldiers going through two and a half months of combat medic training. Only sixteen of us were going on to another eight months of respiratory therapy training. There were six of us male R.T.'s coming from Georgia, and we knew that whatever females had signed up for RT training would meet us there in Texas, so we kept an eager eye out to meet them. They arrived in Texas one day after us.

So here is me up to that point: I have never had a girl-friend, and I could count the number of dates I'd been on without taking off my shoes. I've never kissed a girl, or even held hands with a girl. My plans have never even included girls up to that point because I wanted to do my missionary and military service first. However, with 1.24 of those goals accomplished, I was getting to a point where I would have to acknowledge women. In fact, I had always wanted a wife and a family, so I was less than a year away from actually having to try and impress a girl enough that she would agree to marry me. I was beginning to get nervous. It is what I had worked and planned for, but so far all attempts at communication with the opposite sex had been less than successful, so I wasn't sure how it was all going to play out.

This is where Kelly enters the story. She was one of the female R.T.'s that arrived the day after us. The Army doesn't give trainees much time to socialize during the day, so we Benning boys didn't get a chance to say hi to our female classmates until that evening. Every training day ended the same way—everyone sitting outside of the barracks under the shade of the CTA (covered training area) shining their boots for the next day. Shining boots was mandatory, and shining boots in the barracks was absolutely forbidden, so everyone was guaranteed to be there (under the CTA) at some point during the evening, and that is where we knew we could meet the newly arrived RT girls.

When we were released from duty, my comrades and I quickly ran up to the male barracks to change into our exercise uniforms (shorts, t-shirt, and running shoes) and grab our shoe polishing kits. When we came down with our boots and polish, we spotted our targets already gathered in a circle with their boots. We headed directly over, introduced ourselves, and joined them.

To be honest, my reason for going over to meet those girls was just to get to know my classmates. There were a few cute girls among them, but I didn't really care because I had no expectation of meeting the girl of my dreams in the army. The other guys definitely had intentions, though, and were soon in a contest to draw the most attention to themselves. I figured that the only attention I could draw would be toward the huge dorky glasses I was wearing, so I just kept quiet and off to the side—standard operating procedure for me when it came to women.

Kelly, however, turned out to not be terribly interested in the guys, which caught my attention. It was apparent that she was different than other girls, and so I struck up a conversation with her. It turned out that we both sang our way through basic training (much to the annoyance of our companions), we both loved musicals, and we both hated the same part of "Singing in the Rain." It wasn't much, but that was about the most I had had in common with anyone since I had joined the Army. We talked and laughed until our boots were shined, and then said good-night.

That conversation with Kelly was a refreshing oasis in a cultural desert, and I was whistling all the way to the barracks. I didn't stop whistling until I went to brush my teeth and saw in the mirror that I had a huge shoe polish smear across my nose. An entire half of my nose was black, and it had probably been that way for most of the time I was talking to her. That's what brought me back to the reality that I was a complete dork. I couldn't believe Kelly had talked to me for an hour and had never told me that I had a big black smudge on my face.

Besides the smudge on my face and my face itself, I had a lot of other things working against me. For starters, I was bald, since that is the standard issue Army recruit haircut. I also had on the geekiest glasses you can possibly imagine. If you need glasses in Basic Training, the Army issues what they call BCG's—Birth Control Glasses. These things are *ugly*. They are also nearly indestructible, so that is what you have to wear all the way through boot camp. Most people get rid of them as soon as they graduate from basic training. That was my plan, but the guy on the bunk below me in Texas had forgotten to bring his civilian glasses, so he was stuck wearing BCG's until his mom could mail him his regular glasses. I felt bad for the guy, so I kept wearing my BCG's for the first week so that he wouldn't be the only doofus in the company. So bald, BCG wearing, with a black smudge on my nose was the first impression all of the female R.T.'s (girls with whom I would be spending the next eight months) had of me. It looked like I was well on my way to improving my lady skills. But like I said, it didn't matter because I wasn't really looking for a girlfriend.

Kelly wasn't really looking for a boyfriend, either, but when a cute girl is in a place where the guys outnumber the girls, then she is definitely going to attract some attention, whether she wants it or not. I have to admit that I was interested in her as a friend because we had some shared interests, and I enjoyed talking to her. However, there were several other guys competing for her attention. True to my 'Nice Guy' ways, I kept my distance and watched to see how things played out.

While the other guys vied for her time, I settled for just being in the near vicinity so that I could say hi now and then and observe how things were going. To my amazement, they weren't going. Kelly just wasn't interested in any of the guys. There was one in particular that she shot down in flames because he was being a Jerk.

"What is this?" I thought. "A girl who doesn't care if she's unpopular with the guys?" All of the other girls were pretty much taking advantage of (or being taken advantage of by) the favorable male/female ratio. They liked being such a hot commodity, and the guys were only too eager to play that to their own advantage. But Kelly seemed impervious to the guys' advances, and made it clear that she was not interested. As a result, she quickly dropped off everyone's radar. Except for mine.

I was very intrigued. Kelly was out of the game, and it wasn't because she couldn't compete with the other girls, or that she was too stuck up to consider any of the guys. She voluntarily removed herself because she didn't want the prize. She just wasn't interested, and she couldn't be played. She was just a nice girl…and a smart girl. And the type of girl I had always wished that there were more of.

Now that all of the competition had been eliminated, I got a little braver. I started to arrange things so that I could stand in line next to her. I would sit near her while shining boots, and conveniently forget something from my shoe-shining kit so that I could ask to borrow it from her. I had all sorts of cowardly tricks I used to strike up conversations with her, and then one day, it happened.

I remember it well. I had ended up well ahead of Kelly

in the lunch line, so I had already sat down and started eating when she got her tray. I saw her look around for a place to sit, and she considered sitting with some of the girls she went to boot camp with. But then she saw me at my table, smiled, and *voluntarily* came over to sit with me. Against all odds, my tactics had worked. It turns out that it wasn't really my tactics, nor was it dumb luck. Kelly really was a nice girl, and like me, she liked to take time to survey the people around her before getting into relationships—even friendly ones. She took her time, saw that most of the guys were Jerks, but also noticed me—much the same way I had noticed her. She thought that I seemed like a pretty nice guy, so she decided to get to know me better. That is how we started our friendship.

After combat medic training we moved on to RT training, where the sixteen of us respiratory therapists were put into a single platoon together. That meant that every morning at 4:50 am we were lined up together to exercise, from which we went to breakfast together, then eight hours of class together, then we marched to dinner together, then we would study and shine boots together until 9:30 pm. We were spending almost 17 hours a day with each other. As you might imagine, people's nerves started to wear thin and we started to get tired of one another. However, Kelly and I never ran out of things to talk about, nor did we get tired of talking to each other.

Eventually we earned the privilege of going into town

on the weekends. Everyone else used that opportunity to go to clubs and get drunk. I used it to study and see the sights of San Antonio. So did Kelly. It turned out that she wasn't into drinking and partying, either, so we spent the weekends studying and hanging out together. The funny thing was that while we were anxious to get a break from everyone else on the weekend, we never minded spending the extra time together. And then one day I realized that I looked forward to that time with her.

I couldn't say for sure exactly when it was that things changed, but when I realized that they had I got really scared. Kelly and I were really good friends. Best friends. It didn't really matter if we had something to do on the weekends or not because we just enjoyed talking to each other. Everyone else would take taxis into town, but to save money we would take the bus. The problem was that the nearest bus stop was almost two miles away. So we walked to and from the bus stop every weekend, and talked to each other the whole time. We never minded the walk because we were just happy to be with each other. We were that good of friends, and I was really worried about losing it.

It only took me a week to build up the courage to open the subject for discussion. Other than a lot of 'ums' and 'uhs', I don't really remember what I said, but to my great relief and excitement, she felt the same way. And so we continued being best friends.

It's weird, but nothing really changed. We were already best friends and loved each other, so nothing was different there. Best of all, we had never gone through a phase of pretending to be someone that we weren't. We had always just been ourselves, so there was no insecurity between us. I knew that she knew exactly who I was—good and bad—and she loved me for who I was and not anything else, and vice versa. We weren't putting on a show, and we had no worries of being caught in a lie. I never even saw Kelly wear makeup until we had known each other for six months because she hadn't brought any to training with her. When she went home for Christmas, she brought her make-up back with her. It was weird. I had fallen in love with her while she was wearing baggy camouflage and didn't have her hair done. All of the sudden there she was looking all girly and beautiful. She was stunning—but to this day I think she is most beautiful in the morning before she has had time to do her hair or make-up.

The point is that Kelly and I had just spent the time being the best person each of us knew how to be, and treating each other with kindness and respect because that's how we believed people should be treated. It's who we were. Neither of us had ever planned on falling in love at that moment, but when it happened it all worked out right because we were living life so that it would.

This isn't to say that everything was easy after that. As

friends, all we wanted was to spend time with each other. Now that we were in love…well, we wanted more than that. However, the situation we were in was not exactly the best one for getting married, so we decided to wait— on everything. Before we had met each of us had a firm commitment to wait until marriage to have sex. Now that commitment was being put to the test. Both of us were still determined to live by it, so we made some rules. One of those rules is going to sound real familiar. That's right—NO KISSING!

You probably think we're crazy. We were in love, so why not have sex? What was the big deal? Well, there were a lot of things that made it a big deal, so I'll just explain a couple of the big ones. First, abstinence before marriage is what we believed was right, and neither of us is the sort of person that just sets aside something we believe in because it becomes inconvenient. That's part of what we loved in each other, and we weren't going to ruin that because we couldn't wait a little while.

Second, each of us had a commitment to complete fidelity within our future marriage—which meant that we would only have sex with the person we were married to. That faithfulness was something that extended to even *before* being married. To have sex before being married would be cheating on our future one-and-only. A one-and-only isn't officially a one-and-only until you say "I do," so any sex before marriage, even with each other, would be cheating. We had been loyal to each other our entire lives. Even before we knew each other we had never cheated on each other, and we weren't going to start now.

Third, we knew that temptation would never be greater than it was for that time before we got married. If each of us could stay true to our commitment, it would prove to ourselves and to each other that we could be trusted, and we would never cheat. If I could be abstinent while madly in love with my future wife, then I knew that there would never be a coworker or friend that could make me be unfaithful to my wife later on. If I cheated now, I (and Kelly) would have to question my resolve forever after.

Finally, it was about respect. It was what each of us wanted before we met, and neither of us was going to try and argue or manipulate the other one out of it. We respected each other too much to do that, which is one reason that we have such a great relationship.

With all of that being said, you're probably wondering still why we made the 'no kissing' rule. Like I said before, kissing isn't evil or wrong, but is a gateway to more intimate actions. Frankly, Kelly and I knew that if we started kissing, it wouldn't be long before temptation destroyed all of our resolve and everything we had together. We figured we had at least a year to wait until we could get married, so we better wait on the kissing. This turned out to be wise, because it ended up being five years before we could get married.

"Why," you ask, "did it take five years?" I guess I better finish the story.

After the army, Kelly went back to California, and I went back to New Mexico. We spent a few months in our respective states, and then Kelly moved to Colorado to go to school. Colorado was a whole lot closer than California, but still a fair distance away. So our grand adventures continued. Instead of walking miles together through the bad parts of San Antonio, now we were driving hours to meet each other at the halfway point between us. That halfway point was a rest stop on the side of the freeway in the middle of nowhere Northern New Mexico.

Very romantic, I know. Actually it was a nice little rest stop with covered picnic tables, some trees, and wide-open views of the surrounding countryside. I put my Boy Scout skills to use and planned some very nice picnics. I would load my car with everything needed for a nice candle-lit dinner—food, pots and pans, utensils, camp stove, oil lamps, and checkered table cloths—and leave at about six in the morning so that I could meet her by nine. We would have a simple breakfast together, go on a walk, and then I would make some lunch. We would sit and talk and play games until it started getting dark, which is when I would show off my out-door culinary capabilities and we would enjoy a nice dinner. After dinner we would fire up the laptop and enjoy a movie together before saying good night and driving home.

That was how our long distance courtship proceeded for that semester that she was going to school. Then she decided that before we were married, she would like to spend time as a missionary, also. She worked as a nanny for newborn triplets for a year to save money and then left for Germany for a year and a half.

That was a long time to be apart, but when she returned things fell right back into place. One night I took Kelly on a date and we drove up into the mountains to enjoy the stars as they can only be enjoyed on a pristine mountain night. It was the middle of January, so it was freezing, and it didn't take long before we couldn't feel our ears or noses any more. However, like any adventure Kelly and I took together, frostbite and other little inconveniences were insignificant compared to the pure joy of being together. As we talked, I snuck a ring out of my pocket and slid it onto her finger and asked her to marry me. (This was a tricky feat since my fingers were also going numb by that point, but I managed not to drop the ring.) That night was the first time Kelly and I kissed.

Oh, she said 'yes', by the way.

Soon after we were married, and life has been wonderful every day since then. Even the days that I get thrown up on, or pooped on, or otherwise soiled by our daughter. And I just want to say something about that real quick. Before I was married, I always wished that I was cool. I think pretty much everyone does. Just like pretty much everyone is looking for a person that is cool, and fun, and exciting to date. The problem is that people spend their time looking for that, trying to be that, and going on dates that allow for that.

The problem is, real life has a lot of stuff that just isn't cool, or fun, or exciting. A recent experience dining out with my wife and daughter, who was then about 3 months old, comes to mind. We were with a group of people at a fairly nice restaurant, and we had gotten our drinks and appetizers, and were waiting for our meals to come. I was holding my daughter when she exploded. Literally. I felt the force of it against my chest and looked down to see that my shirt was completely covered in poop. It was so runny that it had gone right through the diaper like it wasn't even there. I had to get up out of the booth and walk out of the restaurant covered in feces. There is no way to be cool while you are doing that. If something like that had happened to me in high school, I would have been mortified—especially if there had been girls around.

I thought of that as I was walking out because I passed a table with several teenage couples sitting at it, and I could see from their faces that they did not think I was very cool. The cool part about it is that my wife and I just laughed it off, without any embarrassment or disdain. We didn't marry each other because we were cool. We married each other because we wanted to face everything in life—from stinky to exciting—together. We married each other for who we really were, not for who we had pretended to be. We married each other because between us we had nothing but trust, respect, love, and kindness. We didn't marry each other for status, convenience, money, or sex. We married each other for "happily ever after."

Endnotes

[1] Reitman, Janet. "Sex & Scanal at Duke." *Rolling Stone* 1 June 2006. http://www.rollingstone.com/news/story/10464110/sex__scandal_at_duke [11 November 2006].

[2] Reitman

[3] Reitman

[4] Reitman

[5] Reitman

[6] Reitman

[7] Reitman

About the Author

Jared Kempton began writing poetry in elementary school, but viewed it as a silly past time—a way of doodling with words. He remembers scoffing at his 9th grade English teacher's comment that he should consider a career in writing. At the time he hated writing anything longer than a five line limerick.

Jared's time in Hong Kong and the army led him back to writing in order to record his experiences, and he has written many unpublished short stories and non-fiction essays. His first published piece appeared in "Miner's Ink", an annual literary volume published at the university he attended.

Jared graduated from New Mexico Institute of Mining and Technology with a degree in Basic Sciences, or (as he likes to say) a B.S. in B.S. and a license to teach it. He currently teaches high school Chemistry and Physics in New Mexico, where he lives with his wife and two daughters.

Looking for more?

Visit my website at www.jaredkempton.com to order copies of this book, get information on events, or to contact me through email.